THE INDIAN ECONOMY

To the memory of P N Mathur
Scholar, colleague and friend

The Indian Economy

Contemporary issues

Edited by
NICHOLAS PERDIKIS
Economics Group
School of Management and Business
University of Wales, Aberystwyth

Routledge
Taylor & Francis Group

LONDON AND NEW YORK

First published 2000 by Ashgate Publishing

Reissued 2018 by Routledge
2 Park Square, Milton Park, Abingdon, Oxon OX14 4RN
711 Third Avenue, New York, NY 10017, USA

Routledge is an imprint of the Taylor & Francis Group, an informa business

Publisher's Note
The publisher has gone to great lengths to ensure the quality of this reprint but points out that some imperfections in the original copies may be apparent.

Disclaimer
The publisher has made every effort to trace copyright holders and welcomes correspondence from those they have been unable to contact.

A Library of Congress record exists under LC control number: 00134002

ISBN 13: 978-1-138-74041-9 (hbk)
ISBN 13: 978-1-138-74040-2 (pbk)
ISBN 13: 978-1-315-18352-7 (ebk)

Contents

PART V   ECONOMIC IDEAS

PART VI   CONCLUSIONS

List of Contributors

T G Arun — Lecturer, School of Public Policy, Economics and Law, University of Ulster.

T Azid — Lecturer, Department of Economics, University of Islamabad.

S P Chakravarty — Senior Lecturer, School of Accounting, Banking and Economics, University of Wales, Bangor.

S Ghatak — Professor of International Economics, The Business School, Kingston University.

D Ghosh — Senior Lecturer, Department of Economics, School of Management, University of Stirling.

J E Hobbs — Assistant Professor, Department of Agricultural Economics, University of Saskatoon.

W A Kerr — Professor of Economics, Department of Economics, Calgary University.

J Kynch — Lecturer, Centre for Development Studies, University of Wales, Swansea.

M Murshed — Lecturer, School of European Studies, Bradford University.

F I Nixon — Professor of Development Economics, School of Economic Studies, University of Manchester.

S Pal — Lecturer, Cardiff Business School, University of Wales, Cardiff.

N Perdikis — Senior Lecturer, Department of Economics, University of Wales, Aberystwyth.

S R C Reddy — Research Fellow, Columbia University, New York.

J U Siddiki — Research Fellow, The Business School, Kingston University.

Foreword

This volume has its genesis in the authors' shared interest in the development of the Indian economy. Our attention was given additional focus by the fiftieth anniversary of India's independence. The Indian economy has been the attention of a great deal of scholarship both since and prior to its independence. This volume attempts to address some of the more contemporary issues that are exercising policy makers and researchers.

Our efforts were greatly assisted by a University of Wales grant which allowed us to meet and exchange views at Gregynog Hall. For his hospitality, assistance and encouragement we would like to thank Dr Dennis Balsom, the Warden of Gregynog Hall.

Many of this volume's contributors were associated with the late Professor P N Mathur, formerly Professor of Economics at the University of Wales, Aberystwyth. As a mark of respect for his many achievements in the field of Economics, his contribution to the study of the Indian Economy, his wisdom and above all his friendship, the contributors dedicate this volume to his memory.

PART I
INTRODUCTION

1 Introduction

N PERDIKIS

While there is no particular theme to this volume the papers do concentrate, in the main, on contemporary issues. For example, trade relations, exchange rate movements, privatisation, labour markets, occupational mobility and poverty and environmental issues. One paper deals with P N Mathur's economic ideas; in particular his contribution to the theory of layers of technique. For ease of presentation the papers are grouped in appropriate parts.

Part two of this volume covers international economic issues. The first contribution by Ghatak and Siddiki examines the emergence and existence of distorted exchange rates in India. The second, by Kerr, Perdikis and Hobbs, discusses the potential for expanding trade between India and the North American Free Trade Area (NAFTA) under a more open trading system. The third in this section by Murshed and Perdikis investigates the development of intra-industry trade between India on the one hand and the UK and EU on the other.

Ghatak and Siddiki begin their paper by outlining India's import substitution programme. This policy supported by a battery of tariffs, quotas and exchange controls had the effect of encouraging a black market in foreign exchange. Despite the economic reform programme begun in the late 1980s and extended in the 1990's the Bank of India still controls foreign exchange transactions strictly. Despite the liberalisation and the consequent reduction of black market premiums in the foreign exchange market controls still remain high. Consequently the costs imposed on the Indian economy are also high. These have been estimated to be in the region of Rs 4.5 billion (World Currency Yearbook 1996). The existence of a black market for foreign exchange can also render the official exchange rate impotent as a policy instrument. To eliminate these costs would require the adoption of a new exchange rate but what value should it have? Ghatak and Siddiki calculate such a rate – the virtual exchange rate (VR) – for India. They do this by estimating the relationship between the official and unofficial black market rate using an autoregressive distributedlag model (ARDL) within a cointegrated system. Ghatak and Siddiki find that for India VRs would be higher than the official rates by 10 per cent in the short run and 16 per cent in the long run but lower than the black market rates.

They conclude that exchange rate distortions are therefore not very severe and can be corrected by the government using appropriate policies. The policy variables identified by the study that would be most effective in eliminating India's foreign exchange distortions are the official exchange rate, interest rate differentials and foreign exchange reserves.

In Chapter 3 Kerr, *et al* look at the effect that India's import substitution programme (based on domestically owned and largely public sector enterprises) had on India-North America trade relations. They find that while India's domestic and foreign economic policies played their role in inhibiting trade, adverse perceptions of India amongst government and business leaders in North America also contributed.

Kerr *et al* argue that the adoption of a more open trading stance since the adoption of the New Economic Policy in 1991 has transformed India-NAFTA economic relations. Trade has been encouraged by the reduction of tariffs and quotas while changes in the rules surrounding foreign ownership, the opening up of previously closed sectors and other institutional reforms have encouraged foreign direct investment.

The creation of NAFTA has also acted as a fillip to trade between India and North America. Not only does it provide India with a new large potential market the adoption of a common set of rules by its members reduced Indian exporters transaction costs when dealing with the North American market. The effect of India's liberalisation has been to increase both exports to and imports from NAFTA. Its exports has largely taken place in manufactures while imports have been biased towards machines and transport equipment. As India's exports have grown faster than its imports her export growth strategy seems to have been vindicated. Total foreign direct investment from NAFTA countries has also increased substantially and with most of it going to so called priority areas this too can be seen as a policy success.

While acknowledging the success of the new policy on trade relations with NAFTA, Kerr, *et al* identify five factors that may inhibit future benefits. These are inadequate infrastructure, concern over intellectual property rights, corruption, India's marginalisation in trade issues and its perceived reticence towards further reform.

Murshed and Perdikis in Chapter 4 continue the theme on India's trade relations. They examine in detail the development of and change in the pattern of trade between India and the European Union. They find that trade between India and its main trading partner has grown substantially especially in the period 1991 to 1996. In contrast to the India - NAFTA picture formal trade links date from early 1963. This was largely stimulated by Britain – then India's principal trading partner – seeking access to the then European Economic Community (EEC). India's fear that successful British entry would cost it tariff free access to its most important market stimulated its desire for a formal agreement. India was successful in its negotiations with the EEC. It gained duty free access for some of its traditional exports such as tea, spices and skins in 1964. This was followed by bilateral agreements on jute and coir and changes to the quotas on silk, cotton fabrics and handicrafts. India became a major beneficiary of the EEC's Generalised Scheme of Preferences when this was established in 1971. These concessions were considered to have given India a major foothold in the EEC. As a result when Britain joined the EEC India was not granted further concessions to protect it from potential losses in the British market. The relationship between India and the EEC did not end there and several formal agreements namely commercial co-operative agreements followed. These were the first of their kind. The original agreement with India was signed in 1973 and was itself superseded in 1983 by one that covered more than just trade issues. A "third generation" agreement signed in 1993 was broader still. The relationship between India and the EU was not without its difficulties both sides accusing the other of unfair trade practices in a number of areas.

The trade pattern between India the EEC and the UK in the early years was of a tradition variety. India exported traditional low-tech products in return for sophisticated manufactures. The pattern began to change by the mid 1990s. While still dominated by inter-industry trade intra-industry trade began to make its appearance. Examining the data by applying recent quantitative techniques reveals that intra-industry trade played an important part in the trade in manufactures (ISTC's 5-8). For trade with the EEC it accounted for thirty per cent and for trade with UK sixteen per cent. Another finding revealed that while intra-industry trade between the EEC and India was growing it remained fairly static with the UK.

The aggregate statistics do though mask some interesting movements within the sub-groups. The major increases took place in Chemicals and Related products (SITC 5) and Machinery and Transport equipment (SITC 7) while Manufactures (SITC 6) and Miscellaneous Manufactures (SITC 8) declined.

Murshed and Perdikis also examine the extent to which intra-industry trade is found in the increase of trade over the period. In other words they examine the extent of marginal intra-industry trade. Using the Brülhart index to measure this phenomenon reveals that the increase in trade between India and its partners was of the inter-industry type. This confirms theoretical expectations although once again examining trade at the individual sector level reveals some exceptions for both trade with the EU and UK.

Murshed and Perdikis also show that India increased its comparative advantage vis a vis both the EU and UK. The exception to this was in manufactures where India was loosing its comparative advantage.

Part 3 deals with industrial policy and environmental issues. In Chapter 5 Arun and Nixon discuss the development of privatisation policy in India, its strengths and shortcomings. They see privatisation in India arising from the failure of the public sector to fulfil its role as an engine of growth. The public sector accounted for half of all industrial investment on which the returns were very low. While providing a positive stimulus to economic growth in the early period of development it eventually became a drain depending on continuous subsidies which exacerbated India's budget deficit. The programme of privatisation begun 1992 when the Government established the Committee on Divestment of shares in Public Sector Enterprises to suggest the best means of implementing a successful privatisation programme. It made a number of recommendations. These dealt with the then nature and process of privatisation, the valuation distribution of shares and how the proceeds should be utilised. While some of the recommendations, in particular those dealing with wider participation were adopted the majority were not. Most significant was the refusal to accept the proposal that majority share holdings should lie in the private sector. Privatisation was thus very limited in the early period. Forty per cent of the companies had divested less than ten per cent of their shares and only ten per cent had divested more than forty per cent. As a result early efforts at privatisation were very limited. By 1995-96 the divestment exercise was disappointing both in terms of the volume of shares in public sector enterprises divested and also in terms of resources realised.

Arun and Nixon's analysis confirms the widely held view that the Indian government was more interested in raising funds to reduce its budget deficit than in having the public sector run efficiently. The limited involvement of foreign companies in the privatisation process can also be taken as an indicator of its lack of success.

Further reforms were undertaken in 1996 through the establishment of a divestment commission to oversee the privatisation process, the main trust was the further encouragement of private participation in the infrastructure sector. As a result deregulation and delicensing have moved on a pace particularly in the power sector and telecommunications.

The success of the privatisation programme in these two sectors and others depends critically on a number of factors. These are the nature of the institutional form of regulations, foreigners' attitudes towards investment in India, its attitudes towards foreign participation and an ingrained belief in the concept of state owned assets.

Chakravarty and Reddy in chapter 6 focus on the international financing of environmental protection in the context of forestry in India. Over half of the assistance for Indian forestry comes from overseas sources. This is usually provided as long term loans, subsidised interest rates and direct grants. Since environmental protection benefits both the recipient and the lenders of funds Indian policy makers are bound to ask the question what share of the costs should they bear? Chakravarty and Reddy question whether the traditional view of conceiving the issue as a game between the donors and the recipient (India) is legitimate.

They identify several reasons for this. Firstly, neither player knows the benefit as perceived by the other player. Secondly, the politicians who enter into negotiations regarding payments are focussed on the short term (electoral cycle) while the benefits accrue long term. As a result politicians concentrate on short run returns rather than long run benefits. To gain advantages in negotiations the parties may well hide their true benefits. Eschewing the game theoretic approach and adopting one based on co-operation Chakravarty and Reddy show that India can gain more by raising international consciousness both at home and abroad. While its share of funds devoted to environmental programmes may decline the absolute amount it gains will increase.

Part 4 deals with poverty in India. The role of occupational mobility on poverty in rural India is examined in Chapter 7 by Pal and Kynch. They argue that occupational mobility may be used as an alternative measure to income and income mobility as a measure of chronic poverty. They attempt to analyse the factors that cause a change of occupation amongst labourers and those that enhance upward mobility. As their test bed they take six villages in East Bengal, all of which reflect regional diversity, different levels of prosperity and patterns of employment.

In their analysis Pal and Kynch identify the factors that determine the desire to change occupation and those that lead to success. Age and the level of schooling affect the former but success depends more on status such as age, sex, caste or socio economic group.

Their study reveals, in line with more traditional work, that zero mobility is the most likely outcome but upward mobility is identified as being determined by sex, age and educational attainment and socio-economic background. It is noted that females have a lower probability of upward mobility along with those (male and female) who are satisfied with their occupation. Those who are members of agricultural labourers households are also less likely to be upwardly mobile than those who are part of an owner occupier or self employed household or where the head is employed in the service sector or works outside the village.

The policy conclusions that Pal and Kynch draw from their analysis is that if poverty is to be alleviated in the rural sector in India barriers to occupational mobility have to be addressed. By identifying the constraints on upward mobility, in contrast to other work, they identify the factors that need targeting in a poverty alleviation policy.

The final paper in the last section of this volume concerns the economic ideas of P N Mathur. Azid and Ghosh trace the development of his economic ideas in a number of areas ranging from Development and Agricultural economics through Input-Output Analysis and layers of technique to his thoughts on problems that were current towards the end of his life. They concentrate, however, on his ideas surrounding the so-called layers of technique discussing in detail his original concepts and their implications. In particular they focus on the development of marginal input output tables, the measurement of total factor productivity and firms entry and exist into and out of an industry.

PART II
INTERNATIONAL ASPECTS

2 Trade Distortions and Virtual Exchange Rates in India

S GHATAK AND J U SIDDIKI

Introduction

It is widely known that the existence of 'dual' rates in the foreign exchange markets – one official and the other 'unofficial' - has important implications for the conduct of exchange rate policy in less developed countries (LDCs) (see, e.g. Dornbusch, 1993; Phylaktis, 1995, for a good review). The two exchange rate markets are separated mainly because of the presence of exchange rate risk premiums, interest rate differentials (foreign and domestic) and expected rate of exchange rate depreciation. Exchange rate distortions can also occur due to government interventions in the foreign exchange market, associated trade controls and mis-invoicing, and problems of moral hazards and adverse selections as perceived by the international lenders to LDCs. Alternatively, chronic and persistent balance of payments problems, presence of trade controls, tariffs and quotas, and financial distortions, such as rapidly accelerating domestic inflation and interest rates vis-a-vis foreign rates, can lead to the emergence of black markets (BM) in exchange rates. These BM rates, if unconnected with the official rates, could render the official exchange rate impotent as an instrument to control the trade balance and foreign exchange reserves. Besides, they impose substantial costs on the economy due to the mis-allocation of resources at both the macro and micro levels, as there are many links between the domestic economy and the rest of the world. The linkage to the goods market can be summarised in terms of the real exchange rate (R) which is the ratio of foreign prices in Rupees to domestic prices in Rupees, i.e.

$$R = \frac{P}{eP^*} \tag{1.1}$$

where 'e' is the nominal exchange rate (Rupees/£), P is the domestic price

11

level, and P* is the foreign price level in pounds. A rise in R (real appreciation) implies that more units of foreign goods are needed to buy one unit of domestic goods. Hence, such a rise in R (real appreciation) implies loss of competitiveness. Alternatively, a decline in R is tantamount to real depreciation and a gain in competitiveness. Thus, the choice of an exchange rate regime can affect a country's competitiveness, trade balance and economic growth.

In general, the asset market linkage shows that for investment in, say, Rupee denominated assets to be competitive, the rupee interest rate i must be greater than the foreign (say £ or $) interest rate, i*, plus the percentage rate of Rupee depreciation, d, i.e.

$$i > i^* + d \qquad (1.2)$$

If equation (1.2) is not satisfied, then there could be capital flight, the loss of reserves and a fall in domestic investment. To differentiate between the domestic and foreign asset markets, capital controls and dual exchange rates have often been used in many East European and LDCs, particularly in Latin America (Charemza and Ghatak, 1990).

Distorted exchange rates drive a wedge between marginal costs and prices and imposes a high tax on the export sector. They also promote rent seeking activities (Krueger, 1974) which often imply large resource costs (both direct and indirect) due to corruption. Moreover, when a country buys foreign exchange at a high price from exporters and sells it at a low price to importers due to dual exchange rates, a budget deficit is almost unavoidable. Such deficits are to be financed either by higher taxes (rather a rare phenomenon in LDCs) or by money creation (a more popular measure). Monetisation of deficits is frequently inflationary (Ghatak and Ghatak, 1996). Thus, exchange rate regimes which are dominated by the BMs could be linked to high inflation. The reduction of such costs due to the presence of BMs in many LDCs provides a strong motivation for attempting to calculate 'virtual' exchange rates – the rate which would have prevailed if the unconstrained import demand were equal to the constraint imposed due to foreign exchange rationing. The elimination of such costs of distortions is a major benefit arising from the measurement and implementation of 'virtual' exchange rates. such 'virtual rates' (VR) can be regarded as 'just bites' of rationed foreign exchange in the sense that the rationed levels coincide with the quantities which would have been chosen by the unrationed agents facing the same prices and income in the Tobin-Houthakker (1950) or Rothbarth (1940) sense. Besides, the costs of attaining/realising the VRs may not be high for some countries.

The paper is organised as follows: In section II, we describe the operations of the MB in foreign exchange in a LDC, i.e. India. In section III, a theoretical model is developed to measure 'virtual' exchange rates which indicates the extent of changes to be made in official exchange rates, thereby reducing if not eliminating, the size of a BM and its costs. Section IV explains the reduced form of the econometric model, data and recently developed autoregressive distributed lag (ARDL) model within a co-integrated system (Persaran *et al*, 1996). In section V, we rigorously analyse the relationship between official and unofficial exchange rates with the aid of the ARDL model within a co-integrated system and report the results obtained for India. The econometric method of measuring VRs are explained and results are reported in section VI. Section VII derives some policy implications and concludes.

BM in Foreign Exchange in India

During the 1950s and 1960s, India launched a major planning programme for rapid industrialisation and economic growth via import substations, tariffs and exchange controls. The main objective was to be economically independent via planning and a policy of import-substitution industrialisation (ISI). Such state interventionist policies were used to insulate the domestic economy from external shocks stemming from the international capital market. Many types of trade controls, coupled with the very high level of effective protection and quantitative restrictions on imports to cure the chronic balance of payments deficits led to the emergence of the black market (BM) and significant exchange rate distortions. Thus, government interventions played a crucial role in the formation of BM rates in India. The determination of the BM premium in LDCs has been the subject of considerable investigation (Dornbusch *et al*, 1983, Blejar, 1978, Agenor 1990, 1991, Charemza and Ghatak, 1990 and Culbertson, 1985, 1989, Mercedo, 1982, 1987).

India approached the end of the 1980s engaged in a reform programme engineered by the late Prime Minister Rajiv Gandhi and his advisors in the early eighties, which aimed to invigorate the country's economic growth rate through economic liberalisation and 'lift the fee of socialist corruption and mismanagement off the neck of the economy'. One of the major planks of the 'New Economic Policy' was to reduce the trade controls via reduction of the tariffs and import controls and a subsequent reduction in the distortions in the exchange rates via devaluation. Table 1 illustrates the changes. They clearly show the high level of the BM premium in the foreign exchange rates in the fifties and the sixties, exhibiting only a gradual reduction in the 1970s and 1980s.

Since independence in 1947, India followed a set of Import Substitution Industrialisation Policies (ISI), until the late 1970s to achieve the national self-reliance. Large scale industries were mainly promoted by planning and regulated by the government. Imports were severely controlled while exports were taxed in various ways. These interventions were reduced in 1985 and 1991. Even so, import tariffs in India still remain as one of the highest in the world and imports of consumer goods are still restricted even after liberalising trade regime significantly in 1990s (World Bank, 1994, p.224). Similarly, foreign exchange is strictly regulated by the central bank of India (IMF, 1997). Consequently, BM premiums are very high though they continue to decline (see table 1). The real GDP growth rate until the middle 1970s was very low (the so-called 'The Hindu-Rate' of 3.5% p.a.) despite the fact that the savings and investment were about one fifth of its GDP (World Bank, 1994). Export taxes together with ISI policies failed to increase exports as a percentage of GDP. Thus, export growth rates have remained stagnant over the period (see table 1). Similarly, important growth has also been very low. In a developing country like India, import content of capital goods should have been very significant. Hence, a low share and growth rate of imports implies that India has been falling behind in the race for acquiring new technology. This is apparent from the fact that the GDP growth rate over the period until the middle of 1980s was very low, even when investment was about one fifth of the Indian GDP. This low growth with high investment ratios suggests that resources are allocated towards the relatively inefficient productive sectors, as is the case in some other developing countries which followed the ISI policies.

India has been losing a huge amount of foreign exchange through the BM due to controls in its external sector. In fact, restrictions on foreign exchange and international trade created massive illegal BMs in foreign exchange. Foreign exchange losses through BMs are estimated at Rs 4.5 billions annually, from which Rs 3 billions are accounted for by smuggling and RS 1.5 billions occur due to under- and over-invoicing (world currency Yearbook, 1996, p. 436). The volume of illegal trading of hard currencies amounted to about 70 per cent of currency in circulation while the average volume of transactions in the BMs per year is estimated as Rs 100 – Rs 150 billions (World Currency Yearbook, 1996, p.436).

Moreover, the level of foreign investment in India is well below that in other large developing countries. For example, on average, foreign investment in India in the recent past was $200 to 400 millions p.a. whereas the comparable figures are $700 to 1000 millions for Indonesia and $1 to 2 billions for China (World Bank, 1994, p. 223).

A Model of Dual Exchange Rates

It is possible to analyse the existence of dual exchange rates in a foreign exchange markets in a simple way. In Figure 1, we measure exchange rates on the vertical axis and the demand for and supply of foreign exchange on the horizontal axis. If the market clears, G will be the equilibrium exchange rate when D_{LF} is the demand for and S_{LF} is the supply of foreign exchange in the economy. But, in many LDCs, the foreign exchange market can be regarded as imperfect, exhibiting strong evidence of administrative control. Suppose, agents seek to maximise their utility which now depends on two arguments, the price of foreign exchange (E) and the quantity of foreign exchange (Q_L). The agents will be indifferent between some combinations of Q_L and E shown as the indifference curves I_1 and I_2. The budget constraint facing agents is given by the line D_{LF}. Agents optimise by choosing a point like F where the indifference curve is tangent to the budget line. Here the exchange rate E_a is higher than the equilibrium rate E_J in a competitive market and the amount of foreign exchange supplied to meet import demand is also lower $(Q_{UL} < Q_{OL})$. This simple diagram clearly illustrates the emergence of dual rates and the restrictions in the foreign exchange market in a competitive and non-competitive market structure.

Frequently in LDCs foreign exchange constraints operate in the official market (OM) and the unofficial market (UM) acts as a clearing house. In a dual exchange market, agents can purchase a certain quantity of foreign exchange from two markets – official (Q_{OL}) and unofficial (Q_{UL}). Thus the agent's utility function (U) is:

$$U = U[(Q_{OL} + Q_{UL}), \overline{M}] \tag{2.1}$$

with

$$M = E_u Q_{UL} + E_O Q_{OL} + \overline{M} \tag{2.2}$$

where E_u = unofficial market rate of exchange rate

E_O = official market exchange rate
M = initial money endowments.

Initially, we assume that Q_{UL} is constrained to $\overline{Q}_{UL}$. Maximising (3) with (4) gives the Clower-Benassy type of the effective demand function.

Table 1 Some Economic Indicators of India: 1965-1996

Average of period	1965-70	1971-75	1976-80	1981-85	1986-90	1991-96
E_{NO}	7.11	8.13	8.22	10.79	15.21	30.89
E_0	9.52	9.56	11.1	14.04	16.23	24.00
Devaluation of E_0	10.39*	0.82	3.05	6.33	3.86	5.56
E_U	10.94	10.54	9.36	12.5	16.65	32.00
E_{NU}	13.76	12.59	12.63	16.29	17.76	24.82
Devaluation of RE_{NU}	5.83*	-6.75	2.54	8.09	2.52	4.88
BM premium	44.39	31.43	13.78	15.91	9.53	3.70
I	1.37	1.065	1.04	1.17	0.78	0.40
Y	3.60*	0.99	3.86	6.8	7.41	4.49** 6.38***
FERIMP	22.1	19.76	60.63	30.51	22.9	44.78
EXPGDP	3.6	3.91	5.48	4.57	4.92	7.83***
OPENNESS	8.79	8.65	12.1	12.18	11.9	16.58***

E_{NO} - nominal official exchange rates, Rupees per US Dollar; E_0 – real official exchange rates, the ratio of foreign (P^*) to domestic price (P) levels multiplied by E_{NO}; E_{NU} – nominal BM exchange rates, Rupees per US Dollar in the BM; E_U – real exchange rates in the MB, the ratio of P^* to P multiplied by E_{NU}; I – the ratio of foreign (Euro dollar rate) to domestic interest rates (discount rate), FERIMP – the ratio of foreign exchange reserves to imports, EXPGDP – exports as a percentage of GDP, OPENNESS – exports plus imports as a percentage of GDP, premium – the ratio of the difference between nominal BM to official exchange rates, all of the ratios are multiplied by 100, Y – real growth rates of GDP, the wholesale price index with the base year 1990 is used as a deflator.

* sample period 1966-1970; ** sample period 1991-1995; *** sample period 1993-1995.

Source: IFS Yearbook (various issues); Pick's Currency Year Book (various issues) and World Currency Year Book (various issues).

Figure 1 The Existence of Dual Exchange Rates

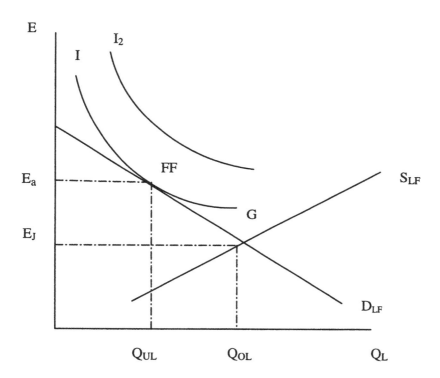

Figure 2 The Virtual Exchange Rate

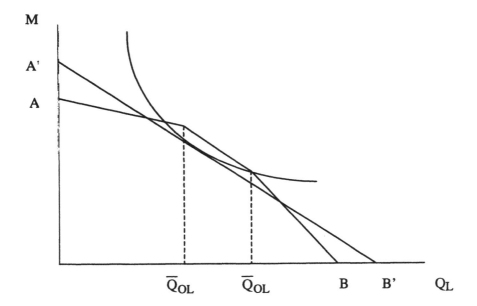

$$Q_{OL} = q_U(E_U, E_O, \overline{M} \tag{2.3}$$

The demand correspondence for the official markets is given by:

$$Q_{UL} = q_u(E_U, E_O, \overline{M}, \overline{Q}_{UL}) \tag{2.4}$$

But given the features of the dual foreign exchange markets, it is useful to assume that Q_{OL} is constrained to $Q_{OL} > \overline{Q}_{OL}$. This yields the equation for the unofficial market exchange rate, E_U.

$$E_U = h(E_O, \overline{Q}_{UL}, \overline{Q}_{OL}, \overline{M}, I) \tag{2.5}$$

The 'virtual' exchange rates, $\underline{E}_v$, then can be defined as (Neary and Roberts, 1980; Charemza, 1990)

$$E_v = \frac{\delta U(.)}{\delta(\overline{Q}_{UL} + \overline{Q}_{OL})} / \frac{\delta U(.)}{\delta M} \tag{2.6}$$

And 'virtual' money as:

$$M_V = M + (E_O - E_V) Q_{OL} + (E_U - E_V) Q_{UL} \tag{2.7}$$

The 'virtual' exchange rate, E_V, is the rate for Q_{OL} and Q_{UL} which supports the quantity $(\overline{Q}_{OL} + \overline{Q}_{UL})$ as a result of quantity unconstraint maximisation for $U = U(Q_{OL} + Q_{UL})$. Figure 2 explains the concepts of 'virtual' prices where M is plotted against the total of $Q_L = (Q_{OL} + Q_{UL})$. As can be seen from figure 2, that the iso-utility curve is not tangent to the budget constraint, because the market is constrained by quantity. Since the importer, under the shortage of Q_{OL}, is at first buying the cheaper product $\overline{Q}_{OL}$, the budget constraint is kinked and given by AB. However, the iso-utility curve is tangent to the line A'B' which shows the budget line under virtual exchange rates with a slope equal to E_V. Thus, E_V, is the price which would have appeared if the unconstrained import demand were equal to constraint imposed.

Econometric Model and Data and Methodology

Econometric Model and Data

From the previous section, following equations (2.5) and (2.6), the long-run model specification for unofficial exchange rates, for a LDC like India, can be written in the following way (all data are in natural logarithms except the ratio of foreign to domestic interest rates):

$$E_U = \alpha_0 + \beta E_O + \gamma Q_{OL} + \delta I + U_t; \text{ with } \beta > 0, \gamma < 0, \delta > 0; \qquad (4.1)$$

E_U – unofficial real exchange rates defined as the ratio of the foreign price level (P^*) to the domestic price level (P) multiplied by nominal unofficial exchange rates, Rupees per Dollar.

E_O – official real exchange rates defined as the ratio of P^* to P multiplied by nominal official exchange rates, Rupees per Dollar.

Q_{OL} – official foreign exchange reserves in US millions dollars used as a proxy of the sum of unofficial and official reserves as a surrogate of monetary instrument (see equation 2). Because unofficial reserves are unobservable

I – ratio of foreign to domestic interest rates[1]
u_t – normally and identically distributed error term

The Methodology

In this paper, we utilise the Autoregressive Distributed Lag (ARDL) method of cointegration analysis recently developed by Pesaran and Shin (1995). The major advantages of this method are that it avoids the requirements of pretesting of the order of integration which is necessary in other cointegration methodologies. That is, the ARDL method of cointegration analysis does not require a knowledge of whether the variables under consideration are I(0) or I(1) (Pesaran and Pesaran, 1997). Moreover, this method avoids the problems of serial correlation that arise in the use of residual-based cointegration methods by an appropriate augmentation (Pesaran *et al*, 1996). The augmented ARDL (p, q_1, q_2 ..., q_k) model can be written as following (Pesaran and Pesaran, 1997, p.397-399):

$$\alpha(L,p)y_t = \alpha_0 + \sum_{i=1}^{k} \beta_i(L,q_i) x_{it} + u_t \tag{4.2}$$

where

$$\alpha(L,p) = 1 - \delta_1 L - \delta_2 L^2 - \dots - \delta_p L^p \tag{4.3}$$

and

$$\beta_i(L,q_i) = \beta_{i0} + \beta_{i1}L + \beta_{i2}L^2 + \dots + \beta_{iq_l} L^{q_l}, \ i = 1, 2, \dots k, \tag{4.4}$$

L is a lag operator such that $L^j y_t = y_{t-j}$, α_0 is a constant, y_t is the dependent variable and x_{it} is the ith independent variables where $i = 1, 2 \dots, k$. The corresponding long-run equation can be written as follows.[2]

$$y = \alpha + \sum_{i=i}^{k} \beta_i x_i + v_t \tag{4.5}$$

where

$$\alpha = \frac{\alpha_0}{\alpha(L,p)}, \beta_i = \frac{\beta_i(L,q)}{\alpha(L,p)} = \frac{\sum_{j=0}^{q} \beta_{ij}}{\alpha(L,p)}, v_t = \frac{u_t}{\alpha(L,p)} \tag{4.6}$$

The error correction representation associated with the ARDL (p, q_1, q_2, $\dots$, q_3) can be written in the following way.[3]

$$y_t = \Delta\alpha_0 - \sum_{j=2}^{p} \hat{\alpha}_j \Delta y_{t-j} + \sum_{i=1}^{k} \hat{\beta}_{i0} \Delta x_{it} - \sum_{i=1}^{k} \sum_{j=2}^{q} \hat{\beta}_{i,t-j} \Delta x_{i,t-j} - \alpha(L,p) ECM_{t-1} + u \tag{4.7}$$

where ECM_t is the error correction term defined as

$$ECM_t = y_t - \alpha - \sum_{i=1}^{k} \hat{\beta}_i x_{it} \tag{4.8}$$

where $\hat{\alpha}_{j,t-j}$ and $\hat{\beta}_{ij,t-j}$ are the coefficients estimated from equation (4.1); and $\alpha(L,p)$ measures the speed of adjustment.

A two-step procedure is used in estimating the long-run relationship (Pesaran *et al*, 1996). In the first step, we investigate the existence of a long-run relationship as predicted by theory between the variables under consideration. If the long-run relationship is supported at the outset, then the long and short-run parameters are estimated in the next stage by using the ARDL method. The first stage can be explained in the following way:

Suppose, we have three variables, y, x and z. Without having any prior information about the direction of the long-run relationship among the variables, we estimate three unrestricted EC regressions where each of the variables is used as a dependent variable in turn. More formally, in the first stages, the following unrestricted error correction model is estimated

$$\Delta y_t = \alpha_0 + \sum_{i=1}^{n} b_{iy}\Delta_i y_{t-i} + \sum_{i=1}^{n} c_{iy}\Delta_i x_{t-i} + \sum_{i=1}^{n} d_{iy}\Delta_i z_{t-i} + \gamma_{1y}y_{t-1} + \gamma_{2y}x_{t-1} + \gamma_{3y}z_{t-1} + \epsilon_t \quad (4.9)$$

The F test can be used for testing the existence of the long-run relationship. The F test for testing the null hypothesis of the 'non-existence of the long-run relationship', i.e. H_0: $\gamma_{1y} = \gamma_{2y} = \gamma_{3y} = 0$, can be denoted by $F(y \mid x, y)$. The $F(y \mid x, y)$ test has a non-standard distribution irrespective of whether variables are I(0) or I(1). The critical values of the F test are computed by Pesaran *et al* (1996) for different numbers of regressors, and whether the ARDL model contains an intercept and/or a trend. Two sets of critical values are computed: One set is based on the assumption that all variables in the ARDL model are I(1) and the other is based on the presumption that all variables are I(0). If the computed F values fall outside the band, a conclusive decision could be drawn without knowing the order of integration of the underlying variables. For example, if the computed F statistic is higher (lower) than the upper bound (lower bound) of the critical value, we would reject (accept) the null hypothesis. On the other hand, if the computed statistic is within the band, information on the order of integration (whether the underlying variables are I(1) or I(0)) is necessary before making decisions regarding the long-run relationship.

Similarly, we could construct the following EC model in which x is the dependent variable:

$$\Delta x_t = \alpha_0 + \sum_{i=1}^{n} b_{ix}\Delta_i y_{t-i} + \sum_{i=1}^{n} c_{ix}\Delta_i x_{t-i} + \sum_{i=1}^{n} d_{ix}\Delta_i z_{t-i} + \gamma_{1x}y_{t-1} + \gamma_{2x}x_{t-1} + \gamma_{3x}z_{t-1} + \epsilon_t \quad (4.10)$$

The F test for testing the null hypothesis of the 'non-existence of the long-run relationship', i.e. H_0: $\gamma_{1x} = \gamma_{2x} = \gamma_{3x} = 0$, is denoted by $F(z \mid y, x)$. Finally, we build the following EC model where z is dependent variable:

$$\Delta z_t = \alpha_0 + \sum_{i=1}^{n} b_{iz}\Delta_i y_{t-i} + \sum_{i=1}^{n} c_{iz}\Delta_i x_{t-i} + \sum_{i=1}^{n} d_{iz}\Delta_i z_{t-i} + \gamma_{1z} y_{t-1} + \gamma_{2z} x_{t-1} + \gamma_{3z} z_{t-1} + \epsilon_t \quad (4.11)$$

The corresponding F test for testing the null hypothesis of the 'non-existence of the long-run relationship', i.e. H_0: $\gamma_{1z} = \gamma_{2z} = \gamma_{3z} = 0$, is denoted by (F(x | y, z). If the empirical analysis shows that the estimated F(y | x, z) is higher than the critical value (upper bound) while F(x | y, z) and F(z | y, x) are lower than the critical value (lower bound), we could argue that there is a 'unique and stable long-run' relationship. In this relationship, y is a dependent variable while x and z are 'long-run forcing' variables.

If a stable long-run relationship is supported buy the first step, then in the second stage, a further two-step procedure to estimate the model (Pesaran *et al*, 1995) is carried out. In the first step of the second stage, the orders of the lags in the ARDL model are selected by Akaike or Schwarz information criteria. In the second step, the selected model is estimated using the OLS method.

Empirical Results

As described above, we follow a two-step procedure to estimate our reduced form structural model, equation (4.1). In the first step, we carried out 'stability tests' for examining the existence of the long-run relationship among the variables E_U, E_O, Q_{OL} and I. The following EC model is constructed where E_U is considered as a dependent variable and E_O, Q_{OL} and I are considered as independent variables:

$$\Delta E_{Ut} = a_{U0} + \sum_{i=1}^{n} b_{iU}\Delta_i E_{U,t-i} + \sum_{i=1}^{n} c_{iU}\Delta_i E_{O,t-i} + \sum_{i=1}^{n} d_{iU}\Delta_i Q_{OL,t=i} + \sum_{i=1}^{n} e_{iU}\Delta_i I_{t-i}$$
$$+ \gamma_{1U} E_{U,t-1} + \gamma_{2U} E_{O,t-1} + \gamma_{3U} Q_{OL,t-1} + \gamma_{4U} It - 1 + \epsilon_t \quad (5.1)$$

Taking into consideration our limited number of observations and annual data, we select n = 2, that is, the number of lags is two[4]. The F test, denoted by $F(E_U|E_O, Q_{OL}, I_t)$, is used to examine existence of the 'stable and long-run relationship'. The null hypothesis of the 'non-existence of the long-run relationship', i.e. the coefficients of all level variables are jointly zero can be written as follows:

$$H_0 : \gamma_{1U} = \gamma_{2U} = \gamma_{3U} = \gamma = 0$$

while the alternative hypothesis that the existence of the long-run stable relationship can be written as

$$H_1 : \gamma_{1U} \neq 0, \gamma_{2U} \neq 0, \gamma_{3U} \neq 0, \gamma_{4U} \neq 0,$$

The calculated F statistic, $F(E_u \mid E_O, Q_{OL}, I_t)$, is equal to 5.03 which is higher than the upper bound critical value 4.378 at a 5% significant level. Therefore, we reject the null of no long-run relationship. Similarly, we constructed another three EC models where E_O, Q_{QL}, I_t, are used as dependent variables in turns (each time). The corresponding F statistics are denoted by $F(E_O \mid E_U, Q_{OL}, I_t)$, $F(Q_{OL} \mid E_U, E_O \, I_t)$, $F(I_t \mid E_U, E_O, Q_{QL}, I_t)$. Our estimated EC models give $F(E_O \mid E_U, Q_{OL}, I_t) = 2.4058$, $F(Q_{OL} \mid E_U, E_O, I_t) = 2.8841$, $F(I_t \mid E_U, E_O, Q_{OL}, I_t) = 2.7578$. These F statistics are lower than the lower bound of the critical value 3.219 at a 5% level. Thus, our results show that only $F(E_U \mid E_O, Q_{OL}, I_t)$ is significant and the remaining $F(E_O \mid E_U, Q_{OL}, I_t)$, $F(Q_{OL} \, E_U, E_O, I_t)$, $F(I_t \mid E_U, E_O, Q_{OL}, I_t)$ are insignificant. Therefore, it is apparent that there exists an unique and stable long-run relationship in which E_U is dependent variables and E_O, Q_{OL} and I are independent variables. Moreover, to find the direction of Granger causality, we run bi-variate VAR models of the first differences of variables. We did not find any support that Granger causality runs from E_U to E_O or to other independent variables[5].

Having found a unique relationship, next step is to select the order of lags in the ARDL model. We estimate the following ARDL (m, n, p, q) model:

$$E_{Ut} = \alpha_0 + \sum_{i=1}^{m} \alpha_i E_{U,t-i} + \sum_{i=0}^{n} \beta_i E_{O,t-i} + \sum_{i=0}^{p} \gamma_i Q_{OL,t-i} + \sum_{i=0}^{q} \delta_i I_{t-i} + u_t \quad (5.2)$$

We selected ARDL (2, 0, 2, 1) model based on the Akaike Information Criterion (AIC). The results of the estimated model are reported in table 2. The corresponding long-run equation of the ARDL model, equation 5,2, can be written in the following way:

$$E_U = \hat{\alpha} + \hat{\beta} E_0 + \hat{\gamma} Q_{0L} + \hat{\delta} I \quad (5.3)$$

where

$$\hat{\alpha} = \frac{\hat{\alpha}_0}{1 - \sum_{i=1}^{2} \hat{\alpha}_i}, \quad \hat{\beta} = \frac{\hat{\beta}_0}{1 - \sum_{i=1}^{2} \hat{\alpha}_i}, \quad \hat{\gamma} = \frac{\sum_{i=0}^{2} \hat{\gamma}_i}{1 - \sum_{i-1}^{2} \hat{\alpha}_i}, \quad \hat{\delta} = \frac{\sum_{i=1}^{1} \hat{\delta}}{1 - \sum_{i=1}^{2} \hat{\alpha}_i}; \qquad (5.4)$$

where hats over the coefficients imply the estimated value from the ARDL (2, 0, 2, 1) model. The estimated long-run equation is reported in table 3. Moreover, the EC representation of the estimated ARDL (2, 0, 2, 1) can be represented in the following way:

$$\begin{aligned}
\Delta E_{Ut} = {} & \hat{\alpha}_0 - \hat{\alpha}_2 \Delta E_{U,t-1} + \hat{\beta}_0 \Delta E_{O,t} + \hat{\gamma}_0 \Delta Q_{OL,t} - 1 + \hat{\delta}_0 \Delta I_t \\
& - \hat{\theta}(E_{U,t-1} - \hat{\alpha} - \hat{\beta}E_{O,t-1} - \hat{\gamma}Q_{OL,t-1} - \hat{\delta}I_{t-1})
\end{aligned} \qquad (5.5)$$

where $\hat{\theta} = (1 - \hat{\alpha}_1 - \hat{\alpha}_2)$ is the adjustment coefficients of the EC mechanisms; $\hat{\alpha}, \hat{\beta}, \hat{\gamma}, \hat{\delta}$, are defined in equation 5.4. The results from the EC representation of the selected ARDL model is reported in table 4.

Table 2   Autogressive Distributed Lag Estimates

ARDL (2, 0, 2, 1) based on the Akaike Information Criterion (AIC)

Dependent variable is E_U

Variables	Coefficient	T-Ratio [Prob]
Constant	.013340	.043012 [.966]
$E_{U\,(t-1)}$	.60743	3.5824 [.002]
$E_{U\,(t-2)}$	-.23862	-1.5027 [.148]
$E_{O,\,t}$	.73430	5.0341 [.000]
$Q_{OL,t}$	-.01	-.017640 [.986]
$Q_{OL\,(t-1)}$	.028761	.44010 [.664]
$Q_{OL\,(t-2)}$	-.075067	-1.5342 [.140]
I_t	.041733	.58286 [.566]
I_{t-1}	.14336	1.9251 [.068]

No. of observation 30; R-Bar-Squared = .90609; DW = 2.1327; S.E. of Regression = .088067 $F_{(8,21)}$ = 35.9747 [.000] Residual Sum of Squares = .16287

Diagnostic Tests

AR2-$F_{(2,\,9)}$ = 0.37 [0.693], AR2-$\lambda^2(2)$ = 1.137 [0.566], RESET-$F_{(1,20)}$ = 3.574 [0.073], NOR-$\lambda^2(2)$ = 0.70 [0.705], H-$\lambda^2(1)$ = 1.9 [0.168], H-$\lambda^2(1)$ = 1.9 [0.168], H-$F_{(1,28)}$ = 1.893 [0.18], E_U-$F_{(2,\,21)}$ = 7.11 [0.004]. E_O-$F_{(1,21)}$ = 25.34 [0.000], Q_{OL}-$F_{(3,\,21)}$ = 1.67 [0.19], I-$F_{(2,21)}$ = 3.52 [0.048]

Table 3 Estimated Long Run Coefficients using the ARDL Approach

ARDL (2, 0, 2, 1) selected based on AIC

Dependent variable is E_U

No. of observation = 30 (from 1967 to 1996)

Variables	Coefficient	T-Ratio [Prob]
Constant	.021134	.043235 [.966]
E_U	1.1633	6.4023 [.000]
Q_{OL}	-.074764	-1.9860 [.060]
I	.29325	2.1450 [.055]

Table 4   Error Correction Representation for the Selected ARDL Model

ARDL (2, 0, 2, 1) selected based on AIC

Dependent variable is E_U

No of observation = 30

Variables	Coefficient	T-Ratio [Prob]
Δ Constant	.013340	.043012 [.966]
$\Delta E_{U\,(t-1)}$	.23862	1.5027 [.147]
$\Delta E_{O,\,t}$	.73430	5.0341 [.000]
$\Delta Q_{OL,\,t}$	-.01	-.017640 [.986]
$\Delta Q_{OL\,t-1}$	.075067	1.5342 [.139]
ΔI_t	.041733	.58286 [.566]
$ECM_{(t-1)}$	-.63119	-4.6857 [.000]

R-Bar-Squared = .51354, S.E. of Regression = .088067
F-Stat. $F_{(6,\,23)}$ = 6.4357 [.000], S.D. of Dependent Variable .12627
Residual Sum of Squares = .16287, DW-statistics = 2.1327

List of Additional temporary variables created:

$\Delta E_{U,\,t} = E_{U,\,t} - \Delta E_{U,\,t-1}$

$\Delta E_{U,\,t-1} = E_{U,\,t-1} - E_{U,\,t-2}$

$\Delta E_{O,\,t} = E_{O,\,t} - E_{O,\,t-1}$

$\Delta Q_{OL,\,t} = Q_{OL,\,t} - Q_{OL,\,t-1}$

$\Delta Q_{OL,\,t-2} = Q_{OL,\,t-1} - Q_{OL,\,t-2}$

$\Delta I_t = I_t - I_{t-1}$

Δ Constant = Constant $-$ Constant$_{t-1}$

$ECM_t = E_{U,\,t} - 1.1633*E_{O,\,t} + 0.074764*Q_{OL,\,t} - 0.29325* I_t - 0.021134*$ Constant

AR2-F is the test for joint autocorrelation of the residuals up to order two. AR2-λ(2) is the chi square statistic for joint autocorrelation of the residuals up to order two. Both of them are insignificant implying that there is no joint autocorrelation of the residuals up to order two. RESET-F is the F test for functional mis-specification which is insignificant denying the possibility of mis-specification, NOR-λ^2(2) is the chi square statistic for testing normality which is insignificant rejecting the possibility of non-normality in error terms. H-λ^2(2) and H-F are the chi square and F statistics, respectively for testing heteroscedasticity. Both of the statistics reject the possibility of heteroscedasticity in error terms. E_U-F, E_O-F, Q_{OL}-F, I-F are F tests for joint significance of the particular variables (contemporaneous and lagged) in the model. For all of the tests in F-form, the degrees of freedom are given in first brackets while the probability is given in square brackets. All variables are significant at less than a 5% level except Q_{OL} based on only the level of significance is not justified. Moreover, Q_{OL} is significant at a 6% level in the static long-run equation.

Our tests on the stability of the model suggest that the model is stable over the sample period (Brown *et al*, 1975). Therefore, we reject the possibility of parameter instability. Besides, the actual and fitted values of the BM exchange rates generally moved together and the residuals of the model were generally within two Standard Error Bands. Thus, the overall fit of the model is very good and it passes all diagnostic tests. (These tests are not reported here but are available for the authors).

The estimated ARDL (2, 0, 2, 1) model reveals that the coefficients of E_O is positive and highly significant implying that official exchange rates have a strong influence on the BM exchange rates. These results support the view that an official depreciation is associated a similar depreciation in the BM rate. An official depreciation generally reduces the BM premiums and the flow supply of forex to the BM through a reduction in the under-invoicing of exports and over-invoicing of imports. This fall in the supply of foreign exchange requires a depreciation in the BM rate to maintain the equilibrium (Agenor, 1990).

The coefficients of I are positive where only lagged I is significant at about 7% level. This finding lends the support to the Dornbusch hypothesis (1993) that the higher the interest rate differentials, the greater the expectations that the domestic currency will be depreciated in the future and hence the demand and price of foreign currencies will be higher in the BM.

Our estimated coefficients of Q_{OL} are not significant and the signs of coefficients on Q_{OL} change in every year. These results can be explained in the following way: the resale of forex obtained from official sources is thought to be one of the major sources of supply of BM foreign exchange. Hence a reduction in supply of forex to the BM at time t, due to the low level of official reserves, increases BM premiums. Consequently, at t+1, there would be an increase in foreign exchange reserves together with high BM premiums. At time t+2, the government starts selling foreign exchange as reserves become higher than demand and hence the economy ends with a low level of reserves and high level of BM premiums at t+3.

The results of the static long-run equation (see table 3) of the ARDL (2, 0, 2, 1) show that all the variables have expected signs. The coefficient of E_O is highly significant emphasising the importance of official exchange rates in the determination of BM rates. Besides, the coefficient of I is positive and significant (at 1 5 per cent level) implying that the larger the interest rate differentials the higher is the BM premium. The policy implication of these findings is that financial liberalisation helps in eliminating BM premiums as it reduces the interest rate differentials. Moreover, the coefficient of Q_{OL} is negative and significant at 5 per cent. These results support the prediction that, in the long-run, a low level of foreign exchange reserves reduces supply of foreign exchange and exerts pressures on the BM and hence increases BM premiums.

The EC model of the selected ARDL model is reported in table 4 which shows that the coefficient of ECM is significantly negative. The variables in first differences represent short-run dynamics while lags of level variables represent the long-run dynamics (Granger, 1988 and Jones and Joulifian ,1991). Hence, the negative coefficient of the ECM implies that the fact that there is a mechanism in the model which prevents the error terms from becoming larger and larger. That is, the BM exchange rate is forced towards the equilibrium defined by the static solution. In terms of short-run dynamics only ΔE_O is individually significant, however, the inclusion of other variables is justified according to the AIC criterion.

Virtual Exchange Rates

In this section, we estimate the VRs from our estimated structural model with the VRs are the prices of foreign exchange which would have appeared if unconstrained import demand were equal to constrained imposed. That is, the VRs equalise E_U to E_O given constrained on other policy variables. The main advantages of this method is that it takes into account of structural relationships among the policy variables. Moreover, this method neither requires a knowledge of the base year (Khan *et al*,

1992) nor does it consider the BM premium as the only indicator of misalignments of exchange rates (Quirk *et al*, 1987).

The estimated version of ARDL (m, n, p, q) model, equation 5.2 reported in table 2, is as follows[6].

$$E_{Ut} = \hat{a}_0 + \sum_{i=1}^{2} \hat{a}_i E_{U,t-i} + \sum_{i=0}^{0} \hat{\beta}_i E_{O,t-i} + \sum_{i=0}^{2} \hat{\gamma}_i Q_{OL,t-i} + \sum_{i=0}^{1} \hat{\delta}_i I_{t-i} + \hat{\mu}_t \quad (5.2')$$

According to the definition, the virtual exchange rate (VR) equates E_U to E_O given the existing constraints on Q_{OL} and I. Hence the estimated short-run ARDL (2, 0, 2, 1) model, equation 5.2', relating E_U to VR can be written as [7]

$$E_{Ut} = \hat{a}_0 + VR_{st} + \sum_{i=0}^{2} \hat{\gamma}_i Q_{OL,t-i} + \sum_{i=0}^{1} \hat{\delta}_i I_{t-i} + \hat{u}_t \quad (6.1)$$

where

$$VR_{st} = \pi_{st} E_{Ot} \text{ with } \pi_t = \sum_{i=1}^{2} \alpha_i + \sum_{i=0}^{0} \beta_0 = (\hat{\alpha}_1 + \alpha_2 + \hat{\beta}_0) \quad (6.2)$$

The short-run virtual exchange rates, VR_{st} can be calculated from table 2, the results of estimated short-run equation 5.2:

$$VR_{st} = \pi_{st} E_{Ot} = = (0.60743 - 0.23862 - 0.73430) E_{Ot} = 1.10223 * E_{Ot} \quad (6.3)$$

Alternatively, we can obtain VR_{st} by taking the weighted average of E_{Ot} and E_{Ut}. That is,

$$VR_{st} = \pi_{st} (\tau E_{Ot} + \mu E_{Ut}) = (\hat{\alpha}_1 + \hat{\alpha}_2 + \hat{\beta}_0)(\tau E_{Ot} + \mu E_{Ut}) \quad (6.4)$$

where τ is the weight given to official rate (E_{Ot}) and μ is the weight given to BM rates (E_{Ut}) such that $\tau + \mu = 1$.

The long-run VR, VR_{Lt}, can be obtained from the estimated long-run equation 5.3 (reported in table 3). The long-run equation (5.3) relating E_U to the long-run virtual exchange rates, VR_{Lt}, can be written as

$$E_U = a + VR_{Lt} E_O + \gamma Q_{OL} + \delta I \qquad (6.5)$$

where

$$VR_{Lt} = \pi_{Lt} E_O = \hat{\beta} E_O = \frac{\hat{\beta}_0}{1 - \sum_{i=1}^{2} \hat{\alpha}_i} E_O = 1.1633\, E_O \qquad (6.6)$$

Alternatively, as in the short-run, we can obtain the VR_{Lt} taking the weighted average of E_O and E_U. That is,

$$VR_L = \pi_{Lt}(\tau E_{Ot} + \mu E_{Ut}) = \hat{\beta}(\tau E_{Ot} + \mu E_{Ut}) = 1.163\,(\tau E_{Ot} + \mu E_{Ut}) \quad (6.4)$$

where $\hat{\beta}$ is defined in equation 5.4 and τ and μ are weights, such that $\tau + \mu = 1$, given to E_O and E_U respectively.

Therefore, the VR rate would be about 10 per cent higher in the short-run and 16 per cent higher in the long-run than the official rates. More interestingly, the VRs are lower than the BM rates indicting the fact that risk premiums are associated with the BM rates. The difference between the VR and BM rates is thought to be positively influenced by the risks associated with BM markets. The risks include the probability of detection (Sheik, 1976) which incurs legal and moral problems. Some summary statistics of official, BM and VRs are given in tables A.1 and A.2 in the appendix.

Conclusions

In this paper, we estimated the interesting concept of 'virtual' exchange rates for India using the recent ARDL method of cointegration analysis. Our results are in accord with the predications of our model. Our analyses reveal that the VRs would be higher than the official exchange rates by about 10 per cent in the short-run, and 16 per cent in the long-run. As the VR is lower than the BM rates, distortions in exchange rates are not very severe and the government can gradually adjust the exchange rates without facing serious difficulties. The VRs are lower than the BM rates indicating the fact that the latter are not equilibrium exchange rates as risk components are included in BM rates.

The linear combination of official exchange rates, foreign exchange reserves and interest rate differentials is cointegrated with BM exchange rates at a 5 per cent significance level and the coefficients of all the variables have expected signs. Therefore, the official exchange rates, interest rate differentials and foreign exchange reserves should be considered jointly as policy variables to eliminate distortions in the foreign exchange market in India.

Our analysis suggests that in India the official exchange rates and interest rate differentials have positive and significant effects on BM exchange rates. An official depreciation generally reduces the BM premiums and hence under-invoicing of exports and over-invoicing of imports which are the main sources of the supply of forex in the BM. Thus, there is a reduction in the flow supply of foreign exchange in the BM. This fall in (flow) supply of foreign exchange requires a depreciation in the BM rate to maintain the equilibrium.

The use of the BM rate as the only guide for adjusting the official exchange rate without knowing the structural relationship among BM and official rates, forex reserves, financial policies is often misleading. In fact, the sign of the MB premiums changes along the adjustment path due to a shock. Thus, our structural model to measure the VRs could be a guide for policy makers in India and in other LDCs to adjust exchange rate misalignments.

The positive and significant coefficient of interest rate differentials supports the Dornbusch hypothesis (1993) that the higher the interest rate differential, the greater the expectations that the domestic currency will be depreciated in the future and hence the demand and price of foreign currencies will be higher in the BM.

Notes

1   The foreign interest rate is proxied by London based Euro Dollar Rate and the domestic interest rate is proxied by Bank Rate, the discount rate given by the central bank to commercial banks.

2   In the long-run steady state, variables do not change and hence we have $y_t = y_{t=1} = y_{t-2} = \cdots y_{t-p}$; $x_{it} = x_{i,t-1} = x_{1,t-2} = \cdots = x_{i,t-q}$ where $x_{i,t-q}$ implies the qth lag of the ith variables.

3   Let,

$$y_t = \Delta y_t + y_{t-1}$$

$$y_{t-m} = y_{t-1} - \sum_{j=2}^{m} \Delta y_{i,t-j-1}, \quad \text{with } m = 2,3,...,p \tag{A.1}$$

and

$$x_{it} = \Delta x_{it} + x_{it-1}$$

$$x_{i,t-m} = x_{i,t-1} - \sum_{j=2}^{m} \Delta x_{i,t-j-1} \quad \text{with } m = 2,3,...,q \tag{A.2}$$

4   Integration and cointegration analyses of the earlier version of this paper show that maximum number of lags is two to avoid the autocorrelation problems. In fact, experience shows that the typical number of lags is two to avoid autocorrelation problems in annual data.

5   The results are available on request.

6   That is, according to the AIC, $m = 2$, $n = 0$, $p = 2$, $q = 1$.

7   For a similar analysis see Charemza (1990) and Charemza and Ghatak (1994).

References

Agenor, Pierre-Richard (1990), 'Stabilisation Policies in Developing Countries with a Parallel Market for Foreign Exchange: A Formal Framework', *IMF Staff Papers*, vol.37, no. 3, pp. 560-592.

Agenor, Pierre-Richard (1991), 'A Monetary Model of the Parallel Market for Foreign Exchange', *Journal of Economic Studies*, vol. 18, no. 4, pp. 4-18.

Blejer, M.L. (1978), 'Exchange Restrictions and the Monetary Approach to the Exchange Rate', in J.A.Frankel and H.G.Johnson (eds), *The Economics of Exchange Rates: Selected Studies*, Reading, MA.

Brown, R., Durbin, J. and Evans, J. (1975), 'Techniques for Testing the Constancy of Regression Relationships over Time', *Journal of Royal Statistical Society, Series B*, vol. 37, pp. 149-172.

Chaemza, W.W. and Ghatak, S. (1990), 'Demand for Money in Dual-Currency Quantity-Constrained Economy: Hungary and Poland, 1956-85', *The Economic Journal*, vol. 100, pp. 1159-1172.

Charemza, W.W. (1990), 'Parallel Markets, Excess Demand and Virtual Prices: An Empirical Approach', *European Economic Review*, vol. 34, pp. 331-339.

Cowitt, Phillips P. (various years), *World Currency Yearbook*, International Currency Analysis, Brooklyn, New York.

Culbertson, W.P. Jr. (1975), 'Purchasing Power Parity and the Black Market Exchange Rates', *Economic Inquiry*, vol. XIII, pp. 250-257.

Culbertson, W.P. Jr. (1989), 'Empirical Regularities in Black Markets for Currency', *World Development*, vol. 17, pp. 1907-1919.

Dornbusch, R. (1993), *Policy Making in the Open Economy*, Oxford University Press, England.

Dornbusch, R., Dantas, D.V., Pechman, C., Rocha, R.R. and D Simoes (1983), 'The Black Market for Dollars in Brazil', *Quarterly Journal of Economics*, vol. 98, pp. 25-40.

Engle, R.F. and Granger, C.W.J. (1987), 'Cointegration and Error Correction: Representation, Estimation and Testing', *Econometrica*, 52, pp. 251-276.

Ghatak, A. and Ghatak, S. (1996), 'Budgetary Deficits and Recardian Equivalence: The Case of India', *Journal of Public Economics*, vol. 60, pp. 267-282.

Granger, C.W.J. (1988), 'Some Recent Development in the Concept of Causality', *Journal of Econometrics*, vol. 39, pp. 199-211.

Gupta. S. (1980), 'An Application of the Monetary Approach to Black Market Exchange Rates', *Welwirtschaftliches Archiv*, vol. 116, pp. 235-252.

Hendry, D.F. (1989), *PC GIVE: An Interactive Modelling System*, Oxford University Press, England.

Hendry, D.F. and Richards, J.F. (1982), 'On the Formulation of Empirical Models of Dynamic Econometrics', *Journal of Econometrics*, vol. 29, no. 3, pp. 3-33.

International Monetary Fund (1997), *Exchange Arrangements and Exchange Restrictions: Annual Report 1997*, Washington, D.C.

Jones, J.D. and Joulifain, D. (1991), 'Federal Government Expenditures and Revenues in the Early Years of the American Republic: Evidence from 1792 to 1860', *Journal of Macroeconomics*, vol. 13, pp. 133-155.

Khan, M.S. and Jonathan, D.O. (1992), 'Response of Equilibrium Real Exchange Rate to Real Disturbance in Developing Countries', *World Development*, vol. 20, pp. 1325-1334.

Krueger, A. (1974), 'The Political Economy of Rent-Seeking Society', *American Economic Review*, vol. 44, pp. 291-303.

Mecedo, J.S., de (1982), 'Exchange Rate Behaviour with Currency Inconvertibility', *Journal of International Economics*, vol. 12, pp. 65-81.

Mecedo, J.S., de (1987), 'Currency Inconvertibility, Trade Taxes and Smuggling', *Journal of Development Economics*, vol. 27, pp. 109-125.

Montiel, Peter J. and Ostry, Jonathan D. (1994), 'The Parallel Market Premium: Is it a Reliable Indictor of Real Exchange Rate Misalignment in Developing Countries?', *IMF Staff Papers*, vol. 41, no. 1, pp. 55-76.

Neary, P. and Roberts, K.W.S. (1980), 'The Theory of Household Behaviour Under Rationing', *European Economic Review*, vol. 13, pp. 25-42.

Pesaran, H.M. and Pesaran, B. (1997), *Microfit 4.0*, Oxford University Press, England.

Pesaran, H.M. and Shin, Y. (1995), 'An Autoregressive Distributed Lag Modelling Approach to Cointegration Analysis', DAE Working Paper Series, No. 9514, Department of Applied Economics, Cambridge University.

Pesaran, H.M., Shin, Y. and Smith, R.J. (1996), 'Testing the Existence of a Long-Run Relationship', DAE Working Paper Series, 9622, Department of Applied Economics, Cambridge University.

Phylaktis, K. (1995), 'Exchange Rate Policies in Developing Countries', in S.Ghatak, *Monetary Economics in Developing Countries*, Macmillan Press Ltd, England.

Pick, F. (Various issues) *Pick's Currency Year Book*, Pick Publishing corporation, New York.

Quirk, Peter J. *et al* (1987), *Floating Exchange Rates in Developing Countries: Experience with Auction and Interbank Markets*, Occasional Paper No. 53, IMF, Washington, DC.

Rothbarth, E. (1940), 'The Measurement of Changes in Real Income under Conditions of Rationing', *Review of Economic Studies*, vol. 8, pp. 100-107.

Sheik, A. Munir (1976), Black Market for Foreign Exchange, Capital Flows and Smuggling', *Journal of Development Economics*, vol. 3, p. 9-26.

Tobin, J. and Houthakker, H.S. (1950), 'The Effects of Rationing on Demand Elasticities', *Review of Economic Studies*, vol. 18, p. 140-153.

World Bank (1994), *Trends in Developing Countries*, Washington, DC.

3 NAFTA and the "New" India

W A KERR, N PERDIKIS AND J E HOBBS

Introduction

Probably the best thing that can be said about economic relations between India and the three countries of North America since the Second World War is that they represent a vast unfulfilled potential. The major reason for this under performance in trade and commercial relations has been the inward focus of India's economic development strategy. Three fundamental principles of India's development strategy set the tone for the country's external commercial relations. The first is that India's industrialisation strategy was based on the import substitution paradigm which had widespread popularity in the 1950s and 60s. Given India's very large domestic market, acceptance of the import substitution paradigm persisted in India much longer than in many other developing countries, primarily because economic growth was never seriously constrained by saturation of the domestic market.

The second principle of India's development strategy which affected its interaction with North American economies was that domestic consumer goods should be produced primarily by domestically owned industries. In effect, this meant that import substitution based consumer product industries were owned and operated by Indian nationals. Strict limits were put on foreign ownership - a maximum of 40 per cent - and a myriad of additional regulatory controls were imposed on foreign investors (Globerman, et. al., 1996). North American industries were, for the most part, shut out of the Indian market. Large transnational corporations were viewed with particular suspicion (Datt, 1995). Of course, as the majority of the world's large transnationals have US origins, the Indian regulatory regime for foreign direct investment was a particular irritant in US-Indian relations.

The third aspect of Indian development strategy which affected foreign economic relations is the large role given the public sector in infrastructure industries such as electric power, transportation and communications as well as basic heavy industries such as iron and steel. 'Foreign investment in the public sector undertakings was not welcomed'

(Patil, 1993, p. 18). A result of the wide range of public sector activities in India was that both for trade and investment opportunities, the US and Canada were shut out of the sectors where they had the greatest comparative advantage during the 1950s, 1960s and 1970s, i.e. machinery and transportation equipment.

The net effect of the latter two principles of India's development strategy was that during the 1980s, foreign direct investment inflows were less than 0.3 per cent of India's gross fixed capital formation, well below the 3 per cent averaged by all developing countries. As the US would have been the major source of foreign direct investment, particularly before the ascendance of Japan in the 1980s, economic relations were significantly curtailed. India, however, put great stock in its *third option* (as opposed to capitalism or communism) and the policy's propositions relating to interactions with the international economy were generally accepted in the government and business and among academics.

It would be wrong, however, to place all the blame for the unrealised potential for mutually beneficial commercial interactions on Indian policies. It would be equally incorrect to treat trade and international commercial policy in the three North American countries as having the same effect on international commerce with India.

Mexico, throughout the 1950s, 1960s and 1970s and well into the 1980s followed an inward looking development strategy that was, in may ways, strikingly similar to India's. Trade was strictly controlled through licensing, and import substitution was the driving force of Mexican trade policy. Foreign investment was treated with suspicion. The public sector was large and was expected to take a leading role in the process of economic development.

Of course, as developing countries, Mexico and Indian produced many of the same goods, and, hence, there was less of a basis for the development of trade links than in the case of Canada and the US. Mexico and India both saw their international comparative advantage deriving from their large quantities of semi-skilled labour. The net result of having similar resource endowments combined with inward looking development strategies was that little trade or commercial interaction developed between Mexico and India.

While the US did chaff under India's trade and foreign investment policies, its general political approach to the South Asian region did little to provide a basis of trust and understanding upon which to build a more co-operative approach to trade relations. As the great global game was played out among the Soviet Union, China and the US, with changing tides and fortunes of the superpowers in the region, the US was often seen by India as a supporter of Pakistan, its regional arch rival. This was particularly true after the Soviet intervention in Afghanistan. Often, the nuances of India's foreign policy in the region were lost on the US. Pakistan, however, was only one of a long string of contentious issues where India and the US differed - Korea, Goa, Vietnam, the Arab-Israeli conflict, the nuclear Non-Proliferation Treaty. The foreign policy of the US toward the region often changed radically as one administration replaced another. While much of the vagaries in US foreign policy can simply be attributed to the low priority given the region, it did not sit well with the government in New Delhi. As Thakur (1996) suggests:

> India used to view the United States as obsessed with anti-communism, insensitive to the precept and practice of non-alignment, prone to relegate Third World countries to the status of pawns on the chessboard of great-power rivalry, prepared to use its global economic clout to ensure hegemony over the Third World, and corrupted by vulgar materialism and hedonism (p. 574).

It is probably not surprising that a basis for improved commercial relations did not arise.

Canada faired much better than the US in terms of India's perceptions of its policies and motives. While of little direct economic substance, the ties to the (British) Commonwealth provided a common basis upon which to build mutual respect and its regularly scheduled meetings provided a forum upon which to build common ground. India perceived itself as a leader of the non-aligned world while Canada often styled itself as a leading middle power. Hence, both countries were often seeking a common middle ground between the superpowers. Canada and India saw eye to eye on issues such as apartheid in South Africa and participated in UN peacekeeping activities. Canada has a relatively large Indian community and was the recipient of a large number of Indian immigrants. This meant considerable interaction between the Indian community in Canada and India.

India's trade and foreign investment policies were, however, equally stringent for the US and Canada and, hence, direct commercial interaction was severely curtailed. Canadian-Indian economic relations were often, as a result, focussed on aid and development assistance. Canada was perceived as being more sensitive to issues which India considered important. Aid projects financed by Canada, for example, were allowed to be executed entirely by Indians (Datt, 1995).

The focus on aid instead of economic interaction on a commercial basis, however, fostered a view in Canada that India was not an equal partner in international commerce. Canadian executives often perceived the Indian economy as one where the level of development precluded, to a large degree, profitable commercial opportunities.

While Indian policy makers formally began to open up the economy in 1985, little real progress was made until 1991 and the announcement of the New Economic (Industrial) Policy. The opening of the Indian economy coincided with a number of events which provided an opportunity to more fully realise the potential gains from increased economic relations between India and North America.

A Changing World

Three major events near the beginning of the 1990s have opened up the possibility for expanded economic relations between the three North American economies and India: (1) the reforms to the Indian economy initiated by the government of Prime Minister P.V. Narasimha Rao in 1991; (2) the signing of the Canada-US Trade Agreement (CUSTA) in 1988 and the subsequent extension of that agreement to include Mexico in the North American Free Trade Agreement (NAFTA) in 1993; and (3) the fall of communism and the disintegration of the Soviet Empire.

While the short run reason for the initiation of reforms aimed at opening up the Indian economy was an acute foreign exchange crisis in early 1991, a more fundamental reason was the poor economic performance of the Indian economy in the 1980s (Storm, 1997). The inward orientation of the development process was seen to have negative consequences. While saturation of the domestic market was not seen as a binding constraint on growth, as had been the case for many developing economies which followed import substitution strategies, the restrictions on foreign participation in the Indian economy was perceived as inhibiting the transfer of technology and the improvement of managerial capability. As a result, India was being left behind in the new *global marketplace* (Patil, 1993). Further, the once vibrant public sector had become excessively bureaucratic and an instrument of social policy rather than economic growth.

> In the early years of independence, the public sector undertaking played an important role in mobilising resources for rapid economic growth as private initiative was weak. Now many of them are running into losses due to lack of initiative, interest, hard work and commitment on the part of employees, frequent strikes, overstaff, etc. (Patil, 1993, p. 20).

Observing the model followed by the Newly Industrialised Countries (NICs) on the Asia-Pacific Rim and latterly, China, export-led growth was perceived as a means to achieve 'faster and more efficient GDP growth through an increase in manufacturing exports' (Storm, 1997, p. 84). Underlying this approach was a major structural change initiative to allow a much greater role for market signals to guide domestic resource allocation. In part, this was to be accomplished through the liberalisation of foreign trade. This was a fundamental move away from planning and bureaucratic decision making as India's resource allocation mechanism.

The reform policy had three major thrusts. On the domestic front, there was to be a move away from state industries toward privatisation. On the international front, there were two initiatives. First, foreign trade was to be liberalised. Tariffs were capped at 65 per cent declining from rates averaging well over 120 per cent and which rose to 400 per cent in some cases (Mishra, 1994). Prior to liberalisation, the World Bank estimated that:

> less than 10 per cent of import categories are subject to less than 100 per cent tariff, about 70 per cent are between 100 and 180 per cent tariff and about 7 per cent are above 200 percent (Mishra, T.K., 1992, p. 49).

By 1996, the import-weighted average tariff was calculated to be 40 per cent (Thakur, 1996). Further, the number of commodities requiring import licences was considerably reduced. The rupee was made fully convertible.

The second aspect of liberalisation in the international sphere was the liberalisation of foreign direct investment laws. The new foreign direct investment package can be summarised as follows: (1) the foreign ownership limit was lifted from 40 per cent to 51 per cent for manufacturing industries, trading companies and banking; (2) foreign technology agreements automatically approved in a set of high priority areas; (3) the establishment of a Foreign Investment Promotions Board for negotiating with multinational corporations bringing single point regulatory clearance; (4) opening up the financial sector to foreign banks; and (5) automatic clearance for capital goods imports (Ghosh and Neogi, 1996). High priority sectors for foreign direct investment include technology consuming industries such as electric power, oil, food processing, chemicals, electronics, telecommunications, transport and industrial machinery (Iqbal, 1994).

On first glance, the formation of NAFTA might not appear to have any significant effect on India's economic relations with NAFTA countries. On the contrary, the NAFTA is a radical shift in the orientation of the three North American economies. In particular, it is concrete evidence of US willingness to pursue trade relations in the middle ground between the multilateral WTO/GATT and bilateral agreements. The Asia-Pacific Economic Conference (APEC) forum and the Free Trade Area of the Americas (FTAA) initiative are other evidence of this openness. The Canadian and Mexican markets add new opportunities to the already large US market.

The opening up of the Mexican market and its domestic deregulation provides both new export opportunities and opportunities for investment. In the case of India, Mexico's accession to the NAFTA may also provide a threat. As the Indian and Mexican economies are similarly structured, India may stand to lose markets in Canada and the US as a result of trade diversion. In a similar fashion, Canadian and US firms may find Mexico more fertile ground for investment than India. As yet, however, it is not possible to discern whether either of these diversions will take place. The difficulties caused by the Mexican peso crisis of the mid-1990s was sufficiently disruptive to trade and investment flows that no trends can be established.

The end of communism in Central and Eastern Europe and the former Soviet Union removed one of the major stumbling blocks to improved relations between the US and India. India's ties to the Soviet Union and its socialist policies were always viewed with suspicion by the US. The USSR actively cultivated India and India blatantly played the US and the USSR off against each other. The obvious failure of planned economies removed this as a serious alternative model for Indian development. Hence, according to Thakur (1996):

> After the 1991 Indian general election, the new Congress government of P.V. Narasimha Rao took note of India's own economic woes and even worse Soviet economics ills, of the dissolution of the Soviet grip on Eastern Europe, of the turmoil in the Soviet Union, and of Americas enhanced global importance in a unipolar world; it concluded that a major improvement in Indo-American relations was required (p. 576).

After 1991, the decks were cleared for expanded relations between India and the NAFTA countries. While the NAFTA countries welcomed India's new openness - it was seen as part of the desirable trend toward more liberal trade regimes in the new global economy - they did not have specific objectives pertaining to Indian-NAFTA trade and commercial relations. India, on the other hand, had two objectives: (1) to increase exports as part of an export-led growth policy; and (2) to attract foreign direct investment to modernise its industry. India had accepted the well known proposition that transnational corporations can be an important conduit for acquiring foreign technology (Kerr and Anderson, 1992). It should be noted, however, that the *openness* pointedly did not include imports of consumer goods. Further:

> There was particular resistance to investment in consumer goods for cultural and economic reasons (Anderson, 1996, p. 173).

Thus, from the Indian viewpoint, success in the new economic relationship with NAFTA countries would be judged on the basis of an increase in export growth relative to import growth, an increase in manufactured exports, an increase in technology imports but not in imports of consumer goods and increases in foreign direct investment in targeted sectors. Of course, if India has been successful, it is unlikely that the NAFTA countries will consider India's new policy regime as a true move to openness.

The Record

Trade between India and the NAFTA countries over the period 1985-1996 is summarised in Table 1. Judged simply by the growth in imports from India and exports to India, it would appear as if India's export-led growth strategy of increased exports combined with limited growth in imports has been achieved. In the case of Canada, between 1990 and 1996 imports from India have increased 128 per cent while Canadian exports to India have actually decreased six per cent. Canadian exports to India increased above 1990 levels in only two years between 1991 and 1996. A similar pattern can be discerned for US trade with India. Imports from India almost doubled over 1990 levels by 1996, while exports to India increased only one-third. Exports to India actually fell below 1990 levels in 1991, 1992, and 1994. Since 1994, when Mexico began opening its economy, the pattern is similar to Canada and the US. Mexican imports from India more than doubled while exports to India decreased. Trade between India and Mexico, however, remains small.

A breakdown of Indian exports to NAFTA countries by industry is presented in Table 2. The major sectors where growth in Indian exports has taken place is in manufactured goods, machines and transport equipment and processed foods. Again, the trade figures would seem to suggest that India's *growth through manufactured exports* strategy is being fulfilled.

India's imports, broken down into industrial classifications, are presented in Table 3. The only significant area of import growth is in machines and transport equipment. This is consistent with the strategy of attempting to improve productivity through the import of technology. Growth in imports of consumer goods is minimal.

While these results may be satisfactory from the Indian point of view - at least in terms of the official development strategy - they are unlikely to be satisfactory from the point of view of the NAFTA countries. The US is particularly sensitive to trade imbalances and has seen its trade deficit with India grow from US$58 million in 1990 to US$237 million in 1996.

The percentage that trade with India constitutes of the NAFTA countries' total trade is presented in Table 4. As can be seen, India remains a minor trading partner for all three countries. In no year did India's share of total imports or exports exceed one percent of the trade of any of the NAFTA countries. While the trends observed in NAFTA-Indian trade may be somewhat disturbing for the NAFTA countries, total trade is simply too small to justify a major confrontation with India.

The foreign investment reforms also seem to be having the effect envisioned by India. The stock of inward foreign direct investment tripled between 1990 and 1995. The largest investors were the United States, Switzerland, Japan and the United Kingdom. India's diaspora have been significant investors (Globerman, et. al., 1996). In the first eight months of 1995, foreign direct investment proposals rose to US$3.08 billion - an increase of almost 50 per cent over the previous year (Anderson, 1996). Iqbal (1994) reports that:

> According to the latest data received by the Reserve Bank of India, more than 90 per cent of total foreign direct investment has gone to high priority areas (p. 131).

Approximately 60 per cent of foreign direct investment comes from the US. What might be more surprising:

> During 1991-92, Mexico had no investment in India. But in 1993, it emerged as the sixth largest investing country (Iqbal and Khan, 1994).

This new interest in foreign markets by Mexican investors reflects the more open attitudes in both India and Mexico.

Canada has also shown considerable interest in investing in the *New India*. Canadian high-technology suppliers, including power generation and telecommunications companies, have secured major contracts in India. Canadian service companies are winning an increasing number of contracts in the consulting sector. A high profile commercial visit by businessmen and politicians led by the Canadian Prime Minister resulted in a large number of contracts being signed between Canadian and Indian firms.

There are approximately 120 Indo-Canadian industrial collaborations. These include edible oil processing, geographic information systems, automotive parts, costume jewellery, aircraft maintenance, poultry breeding and education services. The number of Canadian corporate offices in New Delhi rose from seven in 1988 to twenty-three in 1995.

Canadians were not the only ones involved in high profile visits to India. In January 1995 US Secretary of Commerce, Ron Brown visited India.

> The Brown mission, an example of the Clinton administration's aggressive trade diplomacy in large emerging markets, took place in the wake of a landmark agreement a month earlier opening the huge Indian market to US exports of textiles and clothing. The results of the mission are said to have exceeded expectations, generating deals of around $7 billion in major growth sectors such as telecommunications (exports of US telecommunications equipment to India are expected to grow by 15-20 per cent each year for the next several years), power generation (a 695 MW plant in Maharashtra and a 300 MW plant in Bihar), information systems, and food processing. Apparently, the pre-visit expectation had been for around 2 billion worth of deals. ...The Brown visit was also the occasion for the establishment of a US-India Commercial Alliance to promote trade and investment, which was formally launched in both countries on May 4, 1995 (Thakur, 1996, pp. 580-581).

Transnational corporations based in the US continue to be the most active in India with approximately sixty per cent of foreign direct investment proposals emanating from these companies. In 1993, for example, the value of foreign direct investment proposals from US based transnationals was more than four times those of their nearest rivals, firms from the United Kingdom (Iqbal and Khan, 1994).

Canada and the US have been pleased with these collaborations as opportunities are being created for high technology exports to the long-closed Indian market. These high technology products and services are those in which these two countries perceive their greatest competitive advantage lies.

In general, the record since liberalisation in 1991 would seem to suggest that India's objectives may have been achieved. Export growth to NAFTA markets exceeds, to a considerable degree, the growth in imports from NAFTA countries. Foreign direct investment from NAFTA countries has, for the most part, moved into the technology consuming sectors identified as high priority by the Indian government.

While Indian policy makers may generally be happy with the results of these economic reforms, at least as far as evolving relations with NAFTA countries are concerned, there are a number of emerging difficulties which act to inhibit the benefits available from liberalisation. These will be examined in the next section.

Constraints

Indian-NAFTA economic relationships are faced with five major constraints: (1) inadequate infrastructure; (2) poor protection for intellectual property rights; (3) corruption; (4) marginalisation; and (5) reticence. Marginalisation refers to India's absence as a major player in both multilateral organisations such as the WTO and in regional trade organisations. Reticence refers to the considerable residual suspicion of having too close economic ties with modern market economies. Unless significant progress is made in eliminating or pushing back these constraints, India will not be able to realise fully the potential that the global economy can provide.

Inadequate Infrastructure

Under India's mixed economy model the responsibility for the provision of most infrastructure was given to the state sector. Key sectors required for India's entry into the modern international economy - electrical power generation and distribution, telecommunications, rail transport and highways, ports, airports, heavy transportation equipment and banking were provided by the sector which is broadly recognised as being inefficient, over manned and excessively bureaucratic. These state enterprises *ate up* a large proportion of public revenues with little to show for it. According to the Datt (1995):

> A major cause of inefficiency of the public sector units was bureaucratisation and political interference in decision-making. Another factor contributing to inefficiency was deterioration in work ethics generated by the absolute security of service available to public sector employees (p. 103).

Hence, prior to the start of the reform process in 1991, the Indian public sector was a consistent under performer.

The second major problem with the exclusive public provision of infrastructure was that it did not face private sector competition. If private sector competition had been allowed, newer technology would have been introduced into India's infrastructure by private firms. This would have forced the public sector to update itself. Without competition there was no need to modernise. In particular, if new technologies were labour-saving, they were ignored by public sector providers of infrastructure due to public sector's perceived role as a provider of employment.

The result is that India not only has a telecommunications or rail transportation system which is in inadequate supply, what is supplied is outdated - technology of 1940s vintage or earlier. This level of technological development may have served reasonably well when the Indian economy was closed, but it does not facilitate international economic interaction.

Since 1991, the reform process has opened up much of this previously closed sector to foreign competition or joint venturing. The problem is the enormity of the task. Instead of gradual modernisation, India is faced with replacing almost its entire infrastructure at once, at the same time as trying to expand it to accommodate rapid growth. The task is not simply to add additional infrastructure capacity but to replace much of what already exists.

The magnitude of the task means that to remove the infrastructure constraint large amounts of foreign capital are required. This will require the prospect of large profits for foreign firms. As yet, India does not seem to be willing to pay the price required for the rapid revitalisation of its infrastructure. As Mishra (1994) states:

> These are natural monopolies. Being so it is possible to earn high profits from these naturally protected investments, which is what makes them attractive to foreign investors. India's objective in these areas is to ensure adequate supply of the core sector products at reasonable prices (p. 111).

While these concerns are understandable, it seems unlikely that offering *regulated normal rates of return* will attract sufficient funds to overcome the deficiencies in infrastructure. Increasing competition to eliminate the monopoly position of suppliers would remove some of the objections to foreign investment. While Indian governments at both the national and state level have been willing to allow competition in some areas of infrastructure provision, this is far from universal. In particular, when foreign investors have been invited (allowed) to enter into joint ventures with local infrastructure providers, governments have not been willing to allow the monopoly status of the now joint-venture to lapse. Of course, foreign transnationals would probably not object to having these rents made available through their joint venture partners.

Intellectual Property Rights

The proportion of the value of goods produced in developed countries which is comprised of intellectual property has been rising dramatically since the 1970s (Kerr and Perdikis, 1995). Goods with a high proportion of value derived from intellectual property are those goods where developed countries currently have their greatest competitive advantage. As a result, developed countries have become increasingly concerned with the poor record of intellectual property rights protection in developing countries. One manifestation of this concern was the developed countries insistence that intellectual property rights protection be included in the Uruguay Round GATT negotiations (Yampoin and Kerr, 1996). The result was the Agreement on Trade Related Aspects of Intellectual Property (TRIPs) and the establishment of the New World Trade Organisation (WTO), in part, to administer it.

While intellectual property rights protection in India may not be any worse than in most developing countries, India chose to lead the fight first against intellectual property rights protection being included at the Uruguay Round negotiations and subsequently, to champion a *South* view of intellectual property rights at the negotiations (Patnaik, 1992).

India's high profile stance on intellectual property rights has made foreign firms aware of the difficulties they may face in attempting to protect their intellectual property when entering into joint ventures, franchises and other forms of business arrangements with India firms. Weak intellectual property protection, combined with an ambivalent official position regarding their protection, acts to inhibit foreign investors.

The US, which is a most vociferous advocate of international protection of intellectual property, placed India:

> on the 'Super 301' list in April 1993 for retaliatory trade action if it failed to protect US intellectual property rights (Thakur, 1996, p. 585).

Until India is able to demonstrate that it will implement and effectively enforce its TRIPs commitments, many foreign firms will be wary of investing in India. This will inhibit the process of technology transfer.

Corruption

Corruption raises transaction costs for firms. This is not simply the costs of the bribes themselves, but also encompasses the costs associated with ascertaining the correct official to bribe, assessing the likelihood that the good or service paid for by the bribe will actually be received and determining the appropriate size of the bribe.

It is well recognised that corruption is endemic in India (Roy, 1996). The ability to extract bribes in the international sphere comes primarily from the power to licence economic activity or politically to provide preferred status in tendering for government contracts (Harris-White, 1996). Liberalisation removed some of the ability of bureaucrats to extract bribes by eliminating many of the licences relating to imports and tendering by foreign firms. However, this has meant simply that the point of rent extraction has been displaced.

> While the dismantling of major parts of the old permit, licence, quota raj reduced the power of Indian bureaucratic and political regulators in the old economic ministries, the real action has shifted to the infrastructure ministries. The corridors of Udyog Bhauan (home of the Industries Ministry) may be empty after the dismantling of the 'licence raj' in the manufacturing sector, noted an industrial representative, but the crowd of industrialists, touts and agents has simply shifted to other ministries - power, telecommunications, surface transport, civil aviation and petroleum (Kochanek, 1996, pp. 163-164).

While corruption may be a way of life in India, it is not common in Canada and the US. Businesses from these NAFTA countries find doing business in a corrupt commercial environment very difficult. Dealing with corruption is a skill which needs to be learned. It may be ironic that it is the very transnational corporations, of which India is most fearful, which have the experience to deal effectively with corruption. Many smaller and less internationally experienced NAFTA based firms may simply be deterred from doing business in India. Hence, large transnationals may come to dominate international commercial relations between NAFTA countries and India. Many of the Canadian firms which signed agreements during the Canadian Prime Minister's trade mission to India have complained that nothing came of those agreements due to bureaucratic delays and corruption.

Problems with corruption, hence, have inhibited achieving the full potential of foreign investment. This has two aspects. First, foreign firms are deterred from investing. Second, even if an investment is proposed and approved, it may not come to fruition. According to Iqbal (1994):

> It is believed that only 20 to 25 per cent of the total sanctioned foreign direct investment has reached India (p. 130).

Marginalisation

India is marginalised at both the WTO and in terms of regional trade organisations. The latter are particularly important in the NAFTA context because of the growing importance of regional trade organisations as dynamic forces in the process of trade liberalisation (Yeung et. al., 1997).

India had serious reservations regarding the Uruguay Round Agreements. Hence, while it has signed the Agreements, it is not a major player in the organisation. In any case, India's past stance regarding GATT gives it neither the intellectual nor moral authority to take a leading role.

Not all of India's difficulties, however, are self imposed. India lobbied hard to join both the Association of South East Asian Nations (ASEAN) and the Asia Pacific Economic Co-operation (APEC) forum. Some ASEAN members do not wish the organisation to expand beyond its current geographic confines and it is dealing, rather, with an inter-regional expansion which may include Laos, Cambodia and Myanmar. The inability of India to convince ASEAN's members of its desirability as a trading partner, however, can be seen as a failure in India diplomacy.

In the case of APEC, there is a moratorium on membership which is beyond India's control. Joining APEC would be very important for India's relationships with NAFTA. This is because APEC forms a bridge between ASEAN, Japan, the NICs and NAFTA. Membership would put India in direct contact with NAFTA countries in an organisation which spans the majority of the world's dynamic economies. In some sense, APEC is where the *action* is in global trade relations. Hence, India has been largely sidelined. The South Asian Preferential Trade Agreement (SAPTA) under the auspices of the South Asian Association of Regional Cupertino (SAARC) is limited in its purview and isolated from the dynamism of the Pacific Rim (Anderson, 1996).

Reticence

India is only partially committed to reform. Belief in an inward looking development program - *swadeshi* (economic self-reliance) - is still widespread and the debate over the appropriate development strategy is far from over. As a result, firms from NAFTA countries cannot be assured that the current open policy will not change back to more closed international commercial relations. Further, while politically the need for change may have been accepted:

> disincentive for investment in general, and foreign investment in particular, lies in general apathy of government agencies towards implementing reforms in letter and spirit (Mishra, 1994, p. 112).

Dislike of foreign influences because they are perceived as a threat to the fundamental values of Indian culture is still a powerful idea in India. Anti-foreign sentiment can still garner considerable political support - at least locally:

> In the southern city of Bangalore, a local party threatened to demolish outlets of Kentucky Fried Chicken, claiming that it foists unhealthy living habits on Indians. The BJP government in Delhi closed another Kentucky Fried Chicken for breaches of health regulations, though a court quickly reopened the restaurant (Anderson, 1996, p. 1973).

These and other actions against well known US brands such as Coca-Cola create an impression that India's market is not truly open for business.

Conclusions

Are the constraints outlined in the previous section important? Have they inhibited India's ability to take advantage of trade opportunities with NAFTA countries? There is no easy answer to these questions. One possible way to answer these questions is to compare India's performance since 1991 with that of its great rival as an emerging economy, China. While any comparison must be used with caution, it may also prove instructive. Table 5 compares NAFTA countries' imports from China and India. China has consistently outperformed India in NAFTA markets. In 1985, India's market in the US was almost 60 per cent of China's; in 1996 it was just 12 percent. It would seem clear that China has been much more effective than India in increasing exports to NAFTA countries. A similar story could be told regarding China's ability to attract foreign investment.

China is beset by many of the problems faced by India. If anything, China was more inward looking than India over the post-World War II period. China's infrastructure is also inadequate for a modern economy and obsolete - inhibiting the ability to effectively interact with the modern global economy.   There are also considerable problems with intellectual property protection in China.   Corruption in China is rampant, although it is not as institutionalised as it is in India.   China does not belong to the WTO but does belong to APEC and, hence, is directly involved in a regional trade grouping with the NAFTA nations.

The major difference between China and India may be in the commitment to an open economy.   China seems to have much more enthusiastically embraced the open economy model than India.   This does not mean that foreign transnationals are allowed a free reign in China – China's historical suspicion of foreign influence is well known.   China is simply learning to deal with foreign firms.   Little is heard about threats to Chinese culture.   With the general acceptance of the need to open the economy to foreign investment and trade, the other constraints become manageable.

India may have chosen to take a more cautious approach to openness. The price of this caution is likely much smaller gains from trade and international commercial relations.   If this is a conscious choice, then it may be right for India.   If it is simply a lack of will, then it is truly a missed opportunity.

Table 1   Trade Between India and NAFTA Countries - 1985-96 (millions of US$)

Year	Canada		US		Mexico	
	Imports from India	Exports to India	Imports from India	Exports to India	Imports from India	Exports to India
1985	10.3	30.1	191.2	136.8		
1986	9.9	21.1	190.3	128.0		
1987	10.7	17.3	210.7	122.0		
1988	13.9	26.8	246.0	208.2		
1989	15.8	21.3	276.2	205.3		
1990	16.2	22.6	265.9	207.2		
1991	17.5	21.2	266.4	166.9		
1992	19.3	35.5	315.1	159.5		
1993	22.9	17.5	379.2	230.1		
1994	28.0	16.1	441.8	191.4	4.1	2.7
1995	32.9	26.3	478.0	274.6	5.0	3.1
1996	36.9	21.2	514.1	276.5	10.0	2.0

Source: Monthly Statistics of Foreign Trade, OECD, Paris.

Table 2 Exports of India to NAFTA Countries (millions of US$)

	US		Canada		Mexico	
	1990	1994	1990	1994	1990	1994
Total	342.1	566.3	19.4	33.6	---	13.7
Food & Live Animals	26.5	50.5	2.4	4.5	---	0.2
Beverages & Tobacco	0.2	0.4	---	---	---	---
Crude Materials, Inedible	10.7	13.5	0.4	0.9	---	0.3
Fuel, Lubricants, etc.	29.9	7.0	---	---	---	---
Animal, Veg Oils, Fats, Wax	1.8	3.6	---	---	---	0.1
Chemicals, Related Products Nes	10.4	20.9	0.5	1.5	---	3.1
Manufactured Goods	157.0	242.3	5.6	9.0	---	3.4
Machines, Transport Equipment	8.7	24.4	0.3	1.3	---	2.2
Misc. Manufactured Articles	94.8	201.0	9.9	18.1	---	4.2
Goods Not Classified By Kind	1.7	2.6	0.1	0.2	---	0.1

Source: Commodity Trade Statistics, United Nations, New York.

Table 3 India's Imports from NAFTA Countries (millions of US$)

	US		Canada		Mexico	
	1990	1994	1990	1994	1990	1994
Total	241.1	221.2	27.0	19.2	---	4.1
Food & Live Animals	8.2	8.4	0.6	0.8	---	---
Beverages & Tobacco	0.1	0.1	---	---	---	---
Crude Materials, Inedible	40.8	19.2	9.8	6.3	---	0.1
Fuel, Lubricants, etc.	10.3	4.3	0.3	---	---	---
Animal, Veg Oils, Fats, Wax	1.9	2.6	0.1	0.6	---	---
Chemicals, Related Products Nes	58.8	41.8	3.2	2.7	---	0.3
Manufactured Goods	9.3	12.8	3.2	5.5	---	3.6
Machines, Transport Equipment	79.8	108.6	8.7	2.2	---	0.1
Misc. Manufactured Articles	25.3	17.5	0.6	0.9	---	0.1
Goods Not Classified By Kind	6.3	5.7	0.2	0.1	---	---

Source: Commodity Trade Statistics, United Nations, New York.

Table 4 Trade with India as a Percent of Total Trade - NAFTA Countries

Year	Canada Imports from India	Canada Exports to India	US Imports from India	US Exports to India	Mexico Imports from India	Mexico Exports to India
1985	0.16	0.42	0.66	0.77		
1986	0.14	0.29	0.62	0.71		
1987	0.14	0.22	0.62	0.58		
1988	0.15	0.29	0.67	0.78		
1989	0.16	0.22	0.70	0.68		
1990	0.16	0.21	0.64	0.63		
1991	0.17	0.20	0.65	0.47		
1992	0.18	0.32	0.71	0.43		
1993	0.20	0.15	0.78	0.59		
1994	0.20	0.12	0.80	0.45	0.07	0.06
1995	0.24	0.16	0.77	0.57	0.07	0.06
1996	0.26	0.13	0.78	0.53	0.14	0.04

Source: Monthly Statistics of Foreign Trade, OECD, Paris.

Table 5 Imports from India and China - NAFTA Countries (millions of US$)

Year	Canada		US		Mexico	
	Imports from India	Imports from China	Imports from India	Imports from China	Imports from India	Imports from China
1985	10.3	24.6	191.2	321.8		
1986	9.9	33.9	190.3	397.6		
1987	10.7	48.5	210.7	524.5		
1988	13.9	64.7	246.0	709.4		
1989	15.8	83.3	276.2	994.0		
1990	16.2	99.4	265.9	1,268.7		
1991	17.5	134.9	266.4	1,581.3		
1992	19.3	169.8	315.1	2,139.6		
1993	22.9	199.1	379.2	2,627.9		
1994	28.0	235.2	441.8	3,231.8	4.1	13.0
1995	32.9	282.0	478.0	3,796.3	5.0	16.8
1996	36.9	301.0	514.1	4,291.3	10.0	43.3
% Increase 1991-1996	112.0	123.0	93.0	171.0	---	---
% Increase 1994-1996	32.0	28.0	16.0	33.0	143.00	233.0

Source: Monthly Statistics of Foreign Trade, OECD, Paris.

References

Anderson, W. (1996), 'India in 1995', *Asian Survey*, vol. 36, no. 2, pp. 165-178.

Datt, R. (1995), 'New Economic Reforms - Need for Some Re-thinking', *The Indian Economic Journal*, vol. 42, no. 3, pp. 92-113.

Ghosh, B. and Neogi, C. (1996), 'Liberalisation in India: Quality Differentiates Between Public and Private Employees', *The Developing Economies*, vol. 34, no. 1, pp. 61-79.

Globerman, S., Kokko, A., Revelius, M. and Sami, M. (1996), 'MNE Responses to Economic Liberalisation in a Developing Country: Evidence from India', *Journal of Economic Development*, vol. 21, no. 2, pp. 163-184.

Harris-White, B. (1996), 'Liberalisation and Corruption', *IDS Bulletin*, vol. 27, no. 2, pp. 31-39.

Iqbal, B.A. (1994), 'Will India's External Sector Sustain the Economy?', *India Quarterly*, vol. 50, nos. 1-2, pp. 123-134.

Iqbal, B.A. and Khan, A.O. (1994), 'TCNs: India in a World Perspective', *India Quarterly*, vol. 50, no. 3, pp. 95-102.

Kerr, W.A. and Anderson, C.L. (1992), 'Multinational Corporations, Local Enterprises and the Political Economy of Development - Some Basic Dynamics', *Journal of Economic Development*, vol. 10, no. 1, pp. 105-124.

Kerr, W.A. and Perdikis, N. (1995), *The Economics of International Business*, Chapman and Hall, London.

Kochanek, S.A. (1996), 'Liberalisation and Business Lobbying in India', *Journal of Commonwealth and Contemporary Politics*, vol. 34, no. 3, pp. 155-173.

Mishra, T.K. (1992), 'India's Foreign Trade: Lessons and Challenges', *India Quarterly*, vol. 48, nos. 1-2, pp. 49-58.

Mishra, T.K. (1994), 'Task of Attracting Foreign Investment in India', *India Quarterly*, vol. 50, no. 3, pp. 107-114.

Patil, S.H. (1993), 'Collapse of Communism and Emergence of Global Economy: India's Experiment with New Economic Policy', *India Quarterly*, vol. 49, no. 4, pp. 17-30.

Patnaik, J.K. (1992), 'India and the TRIPs: Some Notes on the Uruguay Round Negotiations', *India Quarterly*, vol. 48, no. 4, pp. 31-42.

Roy, R. (1996), 'State Failure in India: Political-Fiscal Implications of the Black Economy', *IDS Bulletin*, vol. 27, no. 2, pp. 22-30.

Storm, S. (1997), 'Domestic Constraints on Export-Led Growth: A Case Study of India', *Journal of Development Economics*, vol. 52, no. 1, pp. 82-119.

Thakur, R. (1996), 'India and the United States', *Asian Survey*, vol. 36, no. 6, pp. 574-591.

Yampoin, R. and Kerr, W.A. (1996), *Suppressing the New Pirates: Protection of Intellectual Property Rights in Asia - A Challenge for the World Trade Organisation*, EPRI Report, no. 96-01, Excellence in the Pacific Research Institute, University of Lethbridge, Lethbridge, Canada.

Yeung, M., Kerr, W.A. and Perdikis, N. (1997), *Like Ships Passing in the Night: Relations Between ASEAN and the European Union*, EPRI Report No. 97-02, Excellence in the Pacific Research Institute, University of Lethbridge, Lethbridge, Canada.

4 India-European Union Trade Relations and Intra-Industry Trade

M MURSHED AND N PERDIKIS

Introduction

The European Union (EU) is currently India's main trading partner absorbing approximately one quarter of its exports and accounting for roughly the same proportion of its imports. In 1996 total EU-India trade was estimated to be ECUM 18,483 while India's exports to the EU rose by 85.3 per cent in the period 1991 to 1996. Between 1995 and 1996 alone exports grew by 10.2 per cent while imports from the EU grew at a more modest 4.8 per cent.

Traditionally trade between India and Europe and in particular the UK was dominated by trade in different products. On the whole India exported textiles, cotton goods, jute cloth, leather goods as well as commodities such as tea, coffee, cashew nuts, iron ore and manganese. In return India received a whole range of manufactured goods which were not produced domestically. In short the pattern of trade was based on inter-industry trade and typical of that between developed and developing countries.

By the 1970's intra-industry trade - trade in similar goods between countries - had become an important topic in international economics (Grubel and Lloyd 1975). It has been estimated that approximately 60 per cent of all world trade is of the intra-industry type (Greenaway & Milner 1986). The bulk of it is found to exist in trade between developed countries although there is ample evidence to point to its existence in trade between developed and developing countries (Aquino 1978) and between developing nations (Havrylyshyn and Civan 1983).

There are two basic reasons for examining the intra-industry trade patterns between trading partners. The first is simply to document the nature and extent of it and how it has changed over time. This is particularly important in the case of trade between developing and

59

developed countries. Theory suggests that similarity of incomes should play an important role in explaining intra-industry trade (Helpman & Krugman 1983). It is not, therefore, completely clear as to why intra-industry trade should exist between countries with wide differences in income. It could be that countries specialise in the production of goods of different quality. In this way a rich country produces and exports a high quality good to the "rich" in the poor country. The poor country produces and export lower quality goods to the "poor" in the rich country. In this way two way trade in similar goods is established between developed and developing countries.

The second reason is to examine the changes in the intensity of intra-industry trade over time. These so-called marginal changes can help uncover the sort of adjustments taking place in an economy. For instance if the change in trade were of the inter-industry type then the associated expansion or contraction of a particular industry would have substantial consequences for the shedding/take up of labour and capital. For example expansion might be amongst capital intensive industries while contraction could be amongst labour intensive industries. If developments are of the intra-industry type then the displacement of existing factors of production would be less as change would be taking place within the same industry (Brülhart and McAleese 1985). In other words if the trade growth is predominately of the intra-industry variety adjustment costs are lower than they would be under inter-industry trade.

Trade Relations Between India the UK and the European Union

India's economic ties with the UK date back to colonial times and before. It was, though; in the colonial era that formal relations were established and encouraged. In many ways it was the possible loss of access to the UK market that focused India's policy makers minds on the need to establish some form of relationship with the then EEC.

The collapse of Britain's negotiations for entry in to the EEC in 1963 did not mark an end of India's desire to establish formal relations. India sought and achieved the abolition/suspension of import tariffs on bulk tea, spices and skins in 1964. This was followed by bilateral agreements on jute and coir as well as the establishment of duty free quotas on Indian exports of silk and cotton handloom fabrics and handicrafts. When the EEC introduced its Generalised Scheme of Preferences (GSP) in 1971 India became one of the principal beneficiaries.

The relationship between India and the EEC had developed to such an extent that it was felt that India would not be disadvantaged when the UK joined the Community in 1972. No new trading measures were therefore contemplated. In the British-EEC joint declaration of intent issued in 1972 it was though pointed out that steps would be taken to strengthen and expand trade and deal with trade disputes that may arise but little else was envisaged.

In an attempt, however, to rationalise its trade relations with those non-member states that were not covered by either agreements of association on the Lomé convention, the EEC embarked on the development of a series of Commercial Co-operative Agreements. India was the first country to be extended this type of agreement. This was for several reasons. Firstly, India recognised the EEC's economic potential especially as an export outlet for its growing manufacturing sector and was happy with a more formal relationship. Secondly, the EEC also recognised the potential of India as a market for its goods. Thirdly, from the point of view of the EEC there was the possibility that if India signed a Co-operative Agreement then other countries would follow quickly.

The 1973 agreement was superseded in 1983 by a more wide ranging agreement covering, in addition to trade, issues of wider economic significance including industrial, scientific and technical co-operation. By 1990 roughly two thirds of India's exports entered the EEC duty free. The trade relationship was though not always an easy one. India's textile exports to the EEC were subject to the strictures of the Multi-Fibre Agreement (MFA) and the bilateral agreement on textiles signed in 1986.

A so-called "third generation" agreement was negotiated and signed between India and the European Union in 1993. This agreement once again focused on areas of mutual interest in the economic sphere and the enhancement of India's economic development. In particular it emphasised the encouragement of India's policy on trade liberalisation and the encouragement of trade and direct investment between India and the EU. Again the relationship has not been without its friction. For example in 1997 India refused to remove import restrictions on goods entering from the EU citing balance of payments problems as a justification. The EU did not accept this and informally requested consultations under the World Trade Organisations disputes settlement understanding. These duly took place and an agreement was reached concerning agricultural, textile and industrial products. India's import restrictions are to be phased out over a six-year period with a substantial number of particular exports of interest to the EU phased out within the first three years.

It is against this background that we go on to examine the development of intra-industry trade between India and the EU.

Measures of Intra-industry Trade

The most commonly used measure of intra-industry trade is that originally developed by Grubel and Lloyd (1975). It is a measure of the intensity of intra-industry trade and relies on total imports and exports within a particular SITC category:

$$\beta_j = 1 - \left[\frac{|X_j - M_j|}{X_j + M_j} \right] \tag{1}$$

β_j = the measure of IIT - the Grubel and Lloyd index - for each product category j
X_j = value of exports in product category j
M_j = value of importing in product category j.

β_j can range between 0 and 1. The higher β_j the greater the proportion of intra industry trade. The index is independent of the absolute value of exports and imports. The closer β_j is to one the more balanced trade is within a product group. In this way β_j can be high when the total value of intra-industry trade is large or small. Since the numerator is the sum of both exports and imports ($X_j + M_j$) the index is symmetric in the rise in exports and imports, i.e. it can rise as a result of exports or imports or both. The index is, however, non-linear in that a small change in it can hide large changes in the volume of trade. These and other problems such as aggregation and issues dealing with equilibrium are dealt with in Greenaway and Milner (1983).

Marginal intra-industry trade is measured using the Brülhart 1994). This method is very much a counterpart of the Grubel and Lloyd index but deals with the change in trade over time rather than the level of trade at a particular moment. Like the Grubel and Lloyd index it is subject to the same biases, non-linearities and symmetries.

$$A = 1 - \frac{|\Delta X_j - \Delta M_j|}{|\Delta X_j| + |\Delta M_j|} \tag{2}$$

Here Δ denotes the change in the value of trade in a particular product group over a particular period of time. The closer A - the Brülhart index - approaches 1 the greater is the share of IIT in the change in trade between the two time periods. The opposite is the case as the index approaches 0, i.e. the greater the share of inter-industry trade in explaining the growth of bilateral trade in the two periods.

It is possible to attempt to relate the static GL measure with the dynamic Brülhart index. For example as A approaches 1 it indicates that the increase in trade is of the IIT type. If between the two periods the GL index is rising it suggests that trade is also rising. This is because a rise in GL implies more balanced trade or a rise in both imports and exports. The opposite is the case if GL is declining, i.e. total trade must be falling as a falling GL implies a decline in imports and exports (Murshed and Noonan 1996).

As A approaches $\rightarrow$ 0 the implication is that marginal intra industry trade is of the inter industry variety involving adjustment across industries. As rise in GL in these circumstances would suggest that the surplus countries balance would be declining over time which could indicate a decline in comparative advantage or at least a worsening of its trade performance. This is the case because a rising β means that trade is more balanced and if the adjustment is of the inter industry type then there cannot have been a substantial simultaneous rise. The converse would be the case if the GL was declining.

The Extent of Intra-industry Trade

Data

The data pertaining to this work covers the years 1973, 1985 and 1992. In other words the years just after the UK joined the then EEC along with Denmark and Ireland and those that encompassed the further enlargement to include Greece, Spain and Portugal and the beginnings of the 1992 programme. Choosing 1973 means that adjustments to the UK's entry have probably been taken into account. In contrast the further widening of the EEC had little if any effect on the trade volumes as these were and continue to be insignificant both before and after enlargement. It is also unlikely that the 1992 programme or rather the preparations for it had any effect at all.

The study was carried out using data from UN sources - International Commodity Trade Statistics - and conducted at the three-digit level identifying only the sectors in which intra-industry trade existed. All data has been converted to 1992 prices.

Results by Broad Sector

Examining the results in table's 1 and 2 we can see that intra-industry trade is a feature in all product groups bar Category 3 in India-EU trade and categories 3 and 4 in India-UK trade. In other words there is no intra-industry trade in mineral fuels and animal and vegetable fats respectively. For the other categories 5-8 which deal with manufactures intra-industry trade is significant accounting for 30 per cent of trade 1992 with the EU and important in the case of the UK where it accounts for 16 per cent 1992. Interestingly IIT in manufactures has been growing in the case of trade with the EU while it has been fairly static with the UK.

Within manufactures, however, there are some very interesting movements. For example while intra-industry trade has increased in group 5 (chemical and related products) and group 7 (Machinery and Transport Equipment) for the whole period, groups 6 (Manufactures) and 8 (Miscellaneous Manufactures) have declined. In both these last two groups the decline has been substantial from 53 per cent (1973) to 32 per cent (1992) for group 6 and from 21 per cent (1973) to 10 per cent in (1992). It must be said though that the decline for group 6 between 1973 and 1992 does mask an increase between 1985 and 1992 from 27 per cent to 32 per cent.

For the UK the almost static performance of IIT between 1973 and 1992 in manufactures hides fluctuations in some of the categories. For example increases are seen in groups 5 and 7 and declines in 6 and 8.

Even these broad changes also conceal movements within the individual groups at the three-digit level. For instance for India-EU trade in 1973 nine three-digit sub-sectors had GL ratios of over 50 per cent which had risen to seventeen by 1985 and twenty-seven by 1992. For India-UK trade the corresponding figures were eight, nine and forty-three respectively. Once again these are concentrated in the groups 5-8 and particularly 5 and 6, i.e. chemicals and related products and manufactures.

Turning to the measures of marginal intra-industry trade we can see that the increase in trade was mainly of the inter-industry variety for manufactures for both the trade with the EU and the UK but it is more marked for the UK except for sector 7. Again aggregation masks a number of interesting changes at the three-digit level. For trade with the EU seven out of 15 sector 5 categories showed an intra-industry trade increase, three sector 6 categories out of 21, seven sector 7 out of 24 and two sector eight out of 12.

Examining trade with the UK two section 5 subgroups out of eight showed an increase in intra-industry trade, two in sector 6 out of ten, seven sector 7 out of fourteen and three sector 8 out of eight.

Relating the GL and Brülhart measures what can be said? If we look at the broad groupings the results indicate that the EU's trade surplus is declining in sectors 5, 6 and 7. In sector 8 the results indicate a decline in Indian imports and a rise in its overall surplus. Overall for sectors 5 through to 8 the EU's trade surplus with India is worsening/falling.

As far as the UK is concerned the results indicate that the UK's trade surplus is getting smaller in groups 5, 7 and 8. In sector 6 trade is increasing and the UK's surplus is also rising.

Summary and Conclusions

Trade between India and the EU and the UK has been increasing. Traditional theory would suggest that trade would be dominated by the exchange of dissimilar or heterogeneous goods. An examination of the statistics suggests that intra-industry trade plays a part and an important one especially in groups 5-8 - manufactures. Examining trade at the three digit industries reveals that two way trade can be very significant. On the whole, however, the nature of the change in trade in particular between 1985 and 1992 was of the inter-industry type. Once again this was not completely so when trade was examined at the three-digit sub categories. The overall results indicate that India was, however, increasing its comparative advantage which was reflected in the falling deficits with the EU and the UK. Only with trade with the UK in sector 6 goods was India losing its comparative advantage! The overall pattern of adjustment being of the inter-industry variety does suggest that bilateral trade between the EU, UK and India did cause factor displacement.

References

Aquino, A. (1978), 'Intra-industry trade and intra-industry specialisation as concurrent sources of international trade in manufactures', *Weltwirtschaftliches Archiv.* vol. 114.

Brülhart, M. (1994), 'Marginal Intra-industry Trade: Measurement and Relevance for the pattern of adjustment', *Weltwirtschaftliches Archiv.* vol. 130.

Brülhart, M. and McAleese, D. (1995), 'Intra-industry trade and Industrial Adjustment in Ireland', *The Economic and Social Review*, vol. 26, no. 2.

Greenaway, D. and Milner, C. (1986), *The Economics of Intra-industry-trade*, Basil Blackwell, Oxford.

Grubel, H.J. and Lloyd, P.J. (1975), *Intra-industry trade: The Theory and Measurement of International Trade in Differentiated Products*, John Wiley & Sons, New York.

Havrylyshyn, O. and Civan, E. (1983), 'Intra-industry trade and the stage of development', in Tharakan, P.K.M. *Intra-industry trade, Empirical and Methodological Aspects*, Chapter 5, North Holland, Amsterdam.

Helpman, E. and Krugman, P. (1985), *Market Structure and Foreign Trade,* Harvester Wheatsheaf, Brighton.

Murshed, S.M. and Noonan D. (1996), 'The quality and pattern of Intra-Industry Trade between the Geographically Proximate Regions of Northern-Southern Ireland and Southern Ireland and Great Britain', *The Economic and Social Review*, vol. 27, no. 3.

United Nations (1973, 1985, 1992), *International Commodity Trade Statistics*, U.N., New York.

PART III
INDUSTRY AND
ENVIRONMENT

5 Privatisation in India: "miles to go...?"[1]

T G ARUN AND F I NIXON

Introduction

Privatisation is a term which covers a variety of distinct policies, ranging from government disengagement, deregulation and the sale of state owned enterprises and assets to the private sector. The concept of privatisation is not new but the emergence of interest in privatisation since the late 1970s has been the result of a growing disillusionment with the performance of state owned enterprises which in turn has become an integral part of the stabilisation adjustment programs implemented by the international financial institutions.

Since 1991, the Government of India (GOI) has introduced a series of radical economic reforms, including policies of liberalisation, deregulation, disinvestment and privatisation. The underlying rationale of these reforms has been to move from a largely inward-looking interventionist economy to a more open economy that is more responsive to market signals in order to achieve greater efficiency. This paper attempts to take stock of and assess the major issues that have emerged in relation to the experience of privatisation in India during the current decade. The rest of the paper is organised as follows. Section 1 outlines the theoretical issues, methodology and constraints that having a bearing on privatisation. Section 2 analyses the disinvestment of government shares in Public Sector Enterprises (PSEs) in India. Section 3 examines the privatisation programmes in the infrastructure sector particularly with regard to power and telecommunications. Section 4 analyses the regulatory practices of the telecommunications sector in India.

Privatisation: Strategies and Challenges

Just as the 1960s and 1970s were characterised by the rapid expansion of

69

the public sector, the 1980s and 1990s have seen attempts by policy makers to curtail the economic role of the state and to emphasise the promotion of large scale private investment in developmental activities. The PSEs which were expected to produce profits that would then be ploughed back into developmental activities rarely fulfilled this primary objective. Thus in many countries privatisation has been viewed as a means of generating badly needed revenues to scale down budgetary deficits and hence reduce inflationary pressures. Bienen and Waterbury (1989) argue that in most developing countries, privatisation is a response to the need for fiscal austerity and is designed to reduce deficits generated by state owned enterprises. Similarly Rondinelli (1995) points out that that governments in both developed and developing countries have seen privatisation as a means of generating badly needed revenues to reduce budget deficits. This has set the context for restructuring or privatising loss making PSEs in both developed and developing countries.

The neo-classical perspective argues that competitive markets are more effective in achieving an efficient allocation of resources when private property rights are well defined. Property rights theorists (see Furubotn and Pejovich, 1972, for a survey) argue that competition and the transferability of ownership rights in the market place will lead to privately owned resources being employed for the most highly valued uses. Privatisation presupposes that the Government is willing to accept the firm level objective of profit maximisation (Bos, 1991). Thus privatisation is expected to improve the productivity of an enterprise by changing the objectives of the firm, hardening the budget constraint and by superior monitoring (Majumdar and Ahuja, 1997). An ownership change may not, however, deliver increased efficiency and consumer benefits if pre-privatisation restructuring and subsequent regulation fail to create competitive pressures. Vickers and Yarrow (1988) argue that the improvement in the economic performance of privatised firms is not a function of just a change in ownership. The issues of competition and post privatisation regulation are equally important.

In many countries privatisation is treated as the only viable means of creating a system of corporate governance that can overcome the problems of public ownership and make enterprises responsible for costs and profits, thus making them more attractive to capital markets (Rondinelli, 1995). Privatisation is considered in both developed and developing countries as an alternative to expanding state responsibilities for the production and distribution of goods and services.

The three main approaches towards privatisation are: (1) changes in the ownership of an enterprise from the public to the private sector through denationalisation or divestiture; (2) policies involving the liberalisation or deregulation of entry into activities previously restricted to public sector enterprises; and (3) provision of goods or services transferred from the public to the private sector, while government retains ultimate responsibilities for supplying the service (Cook and Kirkpatrick, 1988). Most governments use a combination of these three approaches depending on their objectives, but they need to be aware of the close relationship between the objectives of the privatisation strategy and the techniques that are used for its implementation (Cowan, 1990).

The political impediments to privatisation and the ways by which these obstacles may be eliminated, or at least minimised, is an important issue in formulating privatisation strategies in all countries (Cowan, 1990). The various country experiences support the argument that privatisation strategies and policies often make more sense when interpreted in terms of domestic political considerations. Decisions on privatisation involve a degree of risk in terms of opposition for the government that is directly related to the type of political regime. Cowan (1990) argues that the highest level of risk is seen in a multi-party democratic system in which the ruling party puts its political existence at stake if the privatisation program is not a demonstrable success. This is mainly due to a variety of pressures exerted on a government by opposition parties and different pressure groups such as trades unions and the bureaucracy. For instance, the bureaucracy can derail a carefully planned strategy, discourage potential buyers, and create public suspicion of the government's intentions through a combination of losing files, scheduling endless meetings, and procrastinating in issuing directives (Cowan, 1990). Thus the effectiveness of privatisation and private sector development depends not only on the macroeconomic policy framework but also on the ability of governments to pursue market principles while at the same time reducing the risks of opposition to a politically acceptable level.

Disinvestment of PSEs in India: An Overview

Since independence, Indian development policy has largely been based upon policies of import substituting industrialisation with the aim of creating a mixed economy with a relatively large public sector. The public sector grew from approximately 10 per cent of gross domestic product in 1960-61 to over 25 per cent in the late 1980s. But the PSEs became overall net dissavers and contributed heavily to spiralling budget deficits (Arun and Nixson, 1997). Most of these PSEs survived with government subsidies, and did not have to face the discipline of the market. In addition to owning a large part of the economy, the state also exerted control over the private sector through a variety of regulatory mechanisms.

The economic reforms introduced in 1991 were intended to change this scenario by reducing the heavy reliance on the public sector and encouraging more private sector investment. The Industrial Policy Statement of 1991 stated that the poor performance of public sector enterprises reflected the need for the development of a dynamic private sector[2] (GOI, 1996). But the GOI preferred to use the terms *disinvestment* and *public sector reforms* to privatisation. Whatever the chosen expression however, private participation in economic development emerged as the chosen alternative to the state oriented development strategy.

The GOI began a programme of disinvestment of government holdings in the share capital of selected PSEs in 1991-92. In an attempt to formulate a medium term policy for the disinvestment programme, the GOI established a 'Committee on Disinvestment of Shares in PSEs' in 1992. The Committee was primarily asked to make suggestions on the *modus operandi* of disinvestment to determine the limits on the percentage of equity to be disinvested and to identify the criteria for the valuation of the shares of PSEs. The major recommendations of the Committee were: (1) the need for a medium term action plan instead of yearly targets; (2) preferential offers of shares to workers and employees in public sector enterprises; (3) the formation of an independent regulatory commission; and (4) that ten per cent of the proceeds of disinvestment should be relent to the PSEs on concessional terms to meet the expansion and rationalisation needs.

The recommendations gave a clear direction to the medium term privatisation programme implied by the stated GOI policy towards reforming and restraining the role of the public sector in economic development. Some of the recommendations such as the wider public participation in share holding were incorporated in the 1994 disinvestment programme, but little progress has been made on the major recommendations. In many cases, the GOI preferred to opt for limited disinvestment hoping that the additional measures such as the induction of senior members from the private sector into public sector administration would increase the efficiency of PSEs. It is clear that while the government's shareholding is above 50 per cent, the PSEs will remain under the control of Parliament and they will find it difficult to function as independent profit centres, which may well defeat the basic purpose of the reform process.

The GOI selected 31 public sector enterprises for disinvestment in 1991-92. The number was increased to 40 as of end-September 1996. The majority of these enterprises were in the service sector and in the petroleum and engineering industries. Three companies, Bharat Earthmovers Ltd., Hindustan Organic Chemicals Ltd and Hindustan Petroleum Corporation Ltd had already floated public issues in line with the policy of the Government which encouraged public sector enterprises to access the capital market as appropriate. But the enterprises which had disinvested less than 10 per cent of their shares constituted more than 40 per cent of these forty companies, and only 10 per cent of these companies had disinvested more than 40 per cent of shares. These figures demonstrate the relatively limited magnitude of the disinvestment process so far in India (see Arun and Nixson, 1999 for a detailed discussion).

The criteria adopted in the selection of public sector enterprises and the methods involved in the valuation of shares lacked the essential transparency needed to gain public confidence in the process. There is a view that the shares made available were underpriced in order to ensure that they were sold quickly (Mishra et al., 1993). In a similar tone Sankar et.al (1994, p.84) also argue that 'shares were undersold as a result of a hasty decision'. These analyses show the large differences between the amounts actually realised through disinvestment and the amounts potentially realisable under the best value method. This strengthens the argument that the GOI's basic objective was to use disinvestment to attempt to cover the budget deficit rather than improve public sector performance *per se*. Gouri (1996) has argued that the lack of a clear policy on privatisation and public sector enterprises in India may favour considerations of political expediency in the short run but at the cost of sacrificing sound economic management in the long run.

Another important concern is the minimal participation of foreign investment in the public sector enterprise reforms. It would appear that foreign investors prefer to collaborate with the private rather than the public sector. At the same time, most of the Direct Foreign Investment (DFI) is entering into the core sectors of the economy like telecommunications, oil exploration and power. India has clearly widened the scope for DFI by allowing it into sectors previously reserved for public enterprises (Arun and Nixson, 1997). This raises the hope that more foreign participation in privatisation will be possible in future in line with the experience of privatisation and DFI in other less developed countries.

The formation of the Disinvestment Commission in 1996 gave a new direction to the disinvestment process. The Disinvestment Commission was established with the intention of selling equity in public enterprises to the public, to public enterprise employees, to financial institutions and to overseas investors. The Commission is required to draw up a comprehensive 5-10 year disinvestment programme, ensure transparency in the disinvestment process and oversee the entire disinvestment process; including the amount, price and timing of equity sales, selection of financial advisors; and other matters of detail.

The Commission has published a series of reports, which have criticised the GOI's use of disinvestment as a revenue generation process, rather than aimed at the radical restructuring of the public sector. In February 1997, the Commission raised the issue of funds needed for the revival and restructuring of unprofitable public sector enterprises in the case of eventual disinvestment. It estimated that in 1996-97, the direct burden on the budget on account of unprofitable public sector units was approximately 60 per cent of total direct support to PSEs. Assuming conservatively that this amount would be required annually for the next five years, the total budgetary support worked out at Rs.99.2 billion which discounted at 12 per cent, had a net present value of Rs.72 billion. The Commission felt that this figure needed to be compared with the one-time upfront expenditure needed to restructure and revive loss-making but potentially viable PSEs and the costs of a voluntary retirement scheme to enable closure of the other non-viable PSEs. It was thus observed that if such one-time expenditure was less than Rs.72 billion, it might be financially prudent for the GOI to accelerate the process of disinvestment.

In the same report (February 1997) the Commission outlined its proposals for a long-term strategy on disinvestment, which would revolve around four long-term objectives, viz.: to strengthen PSEs where appropriate in order to facilitate disinvestment; to protect employee interests; to promote broad-based ownership and to augment receipts for the government. The Commission has submitted a number of reports to the GOI, but there appears to be little follow-up action in the form of consultation with the Commission before any steps are taken for disinvestment in PSEs (Arun and Nixson, 1999). In 1998, the GOI removed from the Disinvestment Commission its monitoring role and relegated it to an advisory body without any powers. The statutory status for the Commission might have made disinvestment a meaningful exercise to run PSEs on a commercial basis, but the fact is that by instituting a Commission without executive powers, the GOI has managed to dilute the commitment to disinvestment and radical restructuring of PSEs.

Privatisation in the Infrastructure Sector

The importance of the infrastructure sector as a major contributor to economic growth is now widely accepted[3]. Traditionally, infrastructure has been provided mainly by the public sector both in developed and developing countries and has been monopolistic in nature. It is also characterised by lumpiness in its investments, economies of scale resulting in monopolies, high levels of externalities, intermediate input characteristics, important network effects and difficulties in recovering costs (World Bank, 1992). The awareness of the need for improvements in efficiency and service quality has been pushing many countries towards the privatisation of key activities in the infrastructure sector. As a result, infrastructure-related privatisation dominates the privatisation scenario in the 1990s, capturing more than 40 per cent of proceeds as Governments continued to unload shares in power and telecommunications (Table 1).

Table 1 Privatisation Revenues by Different Sectors in all Countries, 1990-96

Sectors	Revenues (billions of US dollars)	As per cent of Total revenue
Infrastructure	65.34	41.95
Telecommunications	31.28	20.08
Power	19.91	12.78
Manufacturing	37.06	23.79
Primary sector	25.77	16.54
Financial services	22.40	14.38
Other services	5.16	3.3
Total	155.75	100

Source: World Bank, 1998.

In India until the early-1990's, initiatives to implement most infrastructure services were vested in the public sector monopolies. The expenditure on infrastructure was spread thinly across a large number of programs and projects, and paid very little attention to the actual provision of service as opposed to the provision of physical facilities. Inappropriate pricing of infrastructure services and little private sector participation resulted in growing demand-supply gaps, declining rates of cost recovery and inadequate rates of return on investments which discouraged operational efficiency. As part of its reform process, India has deregulated and delicensed the infrastructure sector to a large extent and has opened many areas for private sector participation with the aim of developing an efficient infrastructure and creating a suitable environment for private participation.

Privatisation in the Power Sector

Independence brought into focus the need for accelerating the development of the power supply sector to sustain economic activities and to improve the quality of life of the vast masses of people living in the rural areas. Until then the generation and distribution of electrical power was carried out primarily by private utility companies. Since independence all new power generation, transmission and distribution facilities in the rural sector and in urban centres (which were not served by private utilities) have come under the purview of State and Central Government agencies as a consequence of the concurrent status[4] given by the Constitution to the power sector.

The power sector has made significant progress during the last fifty years. The total generation of electricity increased by almost seventy five times during the 45 years after 1950-51 (Arun and Nixson, 1998b). Thermal plants account for 79.9 per cent of total power generation and hydro electricity plants account for 17.7 per cent, with the balance of 2.4 per cent being generated by nuclear plants (GOI, 1999). But the per capita electricity consumption in India is about 270 kWh per annum which is one of the lowest in the world and is in sharp contrast with the average consumption in the developed countries which is over 5,000 kWh per annum (GOI, 1994b). Moreover, the power sector in India suffers from a number of serious operational problems, including poor quality of services, frequent outages, voltage fluctuations, high system losses and an inadequate transmission and distribution network (World Bank, 1992).

State Electricity Boards (SEBs) generate almost 75 per cent of the country's electricity supply and are responsible for distribution other than for a small segment of the market under the purview of private distribution companies. Although, the Electricity (Supply) Act 1948, stipulates that the SEBs should act as commercially viable organisations[5], in practice, they incur heavy losses on account of highly subsidised tariffs to the agricultural and other domestic consumer groups (Arun and Nixson, 1998b). The relationship between the commercial losses of the SEBs and the subsidies to the agricultural and other domestic consumer groups can be traced from the financial structure of the state power sector (Table 2).

Table 2 Financial Performance of the State Power Sector (Rs.Billions)

	1991-92	1997-98	1998-99 Revenue Estimate
A. Gross Subsidy involved			
(1) On account of sale of			
Electricity to:			
a) Agriculture♦	59.38	190.90	213.21
b) Domestic♦	13.10	51.66	62.62
c) Inter-State Sales♦	2.01	2.58	2.20
Total	74.49	245.15	278.04
(2) Subventions Received			
from State Governments	20.45	72.13	50.71
(3) Net Subsidy	54.04	173.01	227.32
(4) Surplus Generated by sale to			
other sectors	21.73	90.58	96.86
(5) Uncovered Subsidy	32.31	82.43	130.46
B. Commercial Losses@	41.17	118.15	138.07
C. Revenue Mobilisation			
(1) Rate of Return (ROR)❖	-12.7	-19.4	-21.2
(2) Additional Revenue			
Mobilisable from achieving			
a) 3 per cent ROR	49.59	136.46	162.24
b) From introducing 50 paise			
(approximately less than			
one penny)/unit from			
Agriculture/ Irrigation	21.76	27.64	26.70

@ Commercial losses are different from uncovered subsidy because they include financial results of other activities undertaken by the SEBs. (These are excluding subsidy/subvention).
❖ In per cent
♦ This does not include the amount for Delhi except for 1991-92.
Source: GOI, 1999.

The subsidy for the agriculture and domestic sectors has increased from Rs. 72.48 billion in 1991-92 to Rs. 242.56 billion in 1997-98. It is clear (Table 2) that even by charging less than an extra penny per unit of consumption to the agriculture or irrigation sectors, losses could have been reduced to a great extent. But how far such an increase might be possible is a highly complex question in political economy.

This issue has been analysed by Dutt (1997) as a lack of autonomy of the state in relation to society that puts constraints in making policy changes. Dutt further argues that the relationship between the state and the dominant classes is characterised by a certain give and take. The state helps rich and middle-income farmers by supporting food prices, offering subsidies for inputs and through tax breaks. The farmers, in turn, help the parties in control by establishing vote banks given their command over rural votes, and through direct bribes and campaign contributions.

The new power policy permits automatic approval for foreign equity participation of up to 100 per cent for electricity generation, transmission and distribution, for foreign equity investment not exceeding Rs.15 billion (excluding atomic reactor power plants). The foreign owned companies can also set up power projects and repatriate profits without any export obligations. The private power companies have two options. They can operate as generating companies and sell the bulk of their power to the grid without any responsibility for distribution, or they can operate as a licensee wherein they generate their own power and purchases from the SEBs or other generating companies and sell to consumers. The incentives that are offered to the power generating companies include 16 per cent return on equity and 68.5 per cent Plant Load Factor[6] (PLF) for thermal and 90 per cent for hydel and 0.7 per cent return on each incremental one per cent PLF. Incentives for licensees include a valid license for 30 years in the first instance and subsequent renewals for up to 20 years (GOI, 1994b).

The Government decided to do away with the mandatory techno-economic clearances by the Central Electricity Authority (CEA) for power projects with an investment of up to Rs 10 billion and approximately 250 MW capacity. It has been decided to raise the exemption limit for power projects from Rs 4 billion to Rs 10 billion for CEA clearance (GOI, 1997). In 1996, the CEA for the first time issued guidelines to Independent Power Producers (IPPs)[7] on the formulation of comprehensive project proposals, which would enable the CEA to give provisional clearances within thirty days (Arun and Nixson, 1998b).

In an effort to promote private participation and to build the confidence necessary for investors, the GOI has approved counter guarantees in respect of eight fast track private sector power projects. But the GOI has made it clear that the counter guarantees will only be extended where the management of the SEBs as well as the state finances are judged prudent. Though these guarantees increase the confidence levels of lenders in the initial phases, extensive use of them can lead to large liabilities for the Government.

In 1996, the GOI announced a Minimum Plan for Power, which is very ambitious. The policy highlights the importance of a regulatory commission and necessary legislative changes at both the central and state levels in the context of increasing private participation in the power sector. As a result of the policy changes, interest has been expressed in constructing more than 124 power projects with a total capacity of 67281 MW and involving an investment of about Rs. 2464.72 billion. In addition, there are several projects which are being set up by the private sector with the approval of the concerned State Government (GOI 1997). The GOI has been claiming a huge success in the power policy by highlighting the expression of interest by private investors. But progress has otherwise been slow. By 1997, just 11 private projects with a total capacity of 1,892 MW had been commissioned (EIU, 1998).

In reality even many of the 'fast-track' projects lagged behind schedule, due to the endless negotiations, procedural clearance problems and huge delays as illustrated by the case of Cogentrix of the USA (EIU, 1998). The company signed a memorandum of understanding with the Government of Karnataka on the project in 1992 and was one of the eight fast track projects country-wide. In the following year, Cogentrix quoted a cost of Rs 50.28 billion for the plan, and a new company, Mangalore Power Company (MPC) was incorporated. The first PPA was signed with the Government of Karnataka in September 1994, which had forced MPC to reduce the cost to Rs 48.87 billion. Karnataka Electricity Board (KEB) was to buy electricity at Rs 2.54 per kwh. Pressure from the Ministry of Finance, GOI (whose approval of the PPA is mandatory for the counter-guaranteed projects) and an early 1995 reduction in the import duty on coal forced a further reduction in the project cost to Rs 39.84 billion. This necessitated a re-negotiated PPA, which MPC and KEB signed in January 1996 but this was sent to the Finance Ministry, only to be met by new queries and difficulties in April 1997 owing to the national elections and the consequent political confusion. In October 1997, a new and third PPA was signed which provided for a starting tariff of Rs 2.29 per kwh in the year 2000 and a levelised tariff of Rs 1.60 per kwh. After a frustrating delay of five years, Cogentrix officials are reluctant to invest further in India until considerable progress is made in the Mangalore project (EIU, 1998). According to Cogentrix, other markets for power such as China,

Taiwan, the Philippines and Brazil are proving to be equally, if not more, attractive and more competitive because they offer quicker clearances and financial closure.

Since the restoration of the financial health of the SEBs and the improvement in their operational efficiency remains a critical constraint in the development of the power sector, many state governments have initiated reforms in the SEBs. Orissa was the pioneer in this respect. The thermal and hydro generation, transmission and distribution have been corporatised and a State Electricity Regulatory Commission has been set up (See Arun and Nixson,1998b) for the details of Orissa State Electricity Reforms). The experience of the restructuring of Orissa State Electricity Board (OSEB) reaffirms the arguement that any reforms that do not have widespread public support will not succeed[8]. But many of the State Governments are not seen to be very keen to mobilise public support for the reforms, and this may jeopardise the momentum of the reform process. However reforms have been initiated in the states of Orissa, Haryana, Rajasthan, Uttar Pradesh, Bihar and Andhra Pradesh (Arun and Nixson, 1998b).

Regarding private sector participation in the power sector, the World Bank (1996a) observes that a credible government commitment is the fundamental precondition for success. In India, the policy to promote private participation in the development of the power sector has met with the approval of the majority of political parties, but the implementation of these projects raises the need for further reforms in the sector. The Enron episode[9] opens the possibilities of complete privatisation of generation and distribution of power, by permitting private plant operators to sell power directly to consumers, particularly industries, which pay high tariffs. The Government can impose surcharges on every unit sold to industry by the private plant operator and use it for financing the SEBs to provide power to the other groups of consumers (Parikh, 1995). By doing this, the Government can ensure the availability of power to the villages and other weaker sections and groups of society and which will eventually provide a constituency to support the reforms, in turn reducing the degree of political risk.

Privatisation in the Telecommunications Sector

Rapid technological development has led to the dilution in the monopoly nature of ownership in the telecommunications sector both in the developed and developing countries and has reduced the cost of producing, installing and operating transmission and switching equipment (Ambrose,

Hennemeyer and Chapon, 1990). The development of new modes of communication and different value added services has further necessitated wider private sector participation in the telecommunications industry. From this emanates the issue of regulation between the various service providers and the basic network operators in a country. In short, the development of this sector will largely depend on building up (1) diversity of supply and competition (2) participation of private capital and enterprise and (3) effective public regulation (World Bank, 1993).

In India, as with power, telecommunications were a state sector monopoly before 1991. Telecommunications are now recognised as a key area needing rapid growth and massive investment. The New Telecom Policy (NTP) 1994 provided for private sector involvement on an agreed tariff and revenue sharing basis in a bid to make telephone connections available on demand and to raise the standard of services on a par with international levels. The rationale for private sector participation is that the capacity to meet total demand in the industry is beyond the capacity of government funding and the internal generation of resources[10] (GOI, 1994a, para 5 and 6). The NTP envisages the provision of one Public Call office for every 500 persons in the urban areas. According to the NTP, one Village Public Telephone in every village in the country was to be provided by 1997. This target was rescheduled to be met by the end of 2002. The major changes are summarised in Table 3.

The entire telecommunications equipment manufacturing industry has been delicensed and dereserved since 1991. Automatic approval of foreign equity up to 51 per cent has been allowed for foreign investors engaged in the manufacture of all telecommunications equipment. The result has been the tangible growth of telecommunications equipment production since 1991(Arun and Nixson, 1998a). The value-added services in the telecommunications sector were opened up to private investment in July 1992 with the objective of achieving standards comparable to international facilities. The GOI has permitted the companies registered in India to operate under license on a non-exclusive basis in the following services - Electronic Mail, Voice Mail, Data services, Audiotex Services, Videotex Services and Video Conferencing.

The conditions for the operation of private participants include agreed tariff and revenue sharing arrangements, but the 1994 policy does not identify the basis of the upward revision of the demand or the mechanisms through which the private and foreign sectors can participate in the basic telecommunications services. Only companies registered in India will be permitted to participate in providing basic telephone services. In the event of a joint venture, the maximum permissible foreign equity is 49 per cent.

Table 3 Major Changes in the Telecommunications Sector

1991	The tele-communications equipment manufacturing industry de-regulated with automatic approval of foreign equity up to 51 per cent of total equity.
1992	Value added services opened for private sector participation which include Cellular Mobile Telephones, Radio paging, Electronic mail, Voice mail/Audio tex services, Data services, Video-conferencing and Credit card authorisation services.
1994	The Government permitted a maximum foreign equity of 49 per cent in the case of Basic services, Cellular mobile, Radio paging and other wireless services.
1995	The Government permitted a maximum foreign equity of 49 per cent in the case of Basic services, Cellular mobile, Radio paging and other wireless services.
1996	Letters of intent issued to eight selected bidders in twelve circles for providing Basic tele-communications services. Formation of Telecom Regulatory Authority of India (TRAI).
1997	First ruling by TRAI against DoT increase in tariffs on calls from fixed to mobile phones. Government announces modifications of license conditions for provision of basic and cellular mobile telephone services.

Source: GOI, 1997.

The financial bids for basic telecommunication services have been floated three times since 1995. Even after this lengthy process only high revenue earning states have found bidders, whereas in eight states no bids have been received. The bidding process was not free of criticisms. The circles (an administrative entity) which failed to attract competitive bids constituted 33 per cent of the total villages in India (GOI, 1994a, para 3). As rural telephones were the major thrust of the NTP, it is important to note the impact of the lack of bids for these circles. In addition, even though the NTP insisted that the technology brought in by the pilot projects should be state-of-art technology, it seems that this stipulation was diluted in the tender document and not given much weight in the bidding process (see Arun and Nixson (1998a) for the details of the bidding exercise for basic services).

The introduction of the private sector into the telecommunications sector made it necessary for the DoT to alter its structure and operations to become more competitive. The advantages of restructuring the state owned operator prior to privatisation are: (1) successful restructuring will enhance the operator's performance and will help to increase the sale value at the time of privatisation; (2) the successful restructuring program can enhance management and labour productivity and morale, build confidence in the privatisation process and reduce likely objections of employees (World Bank, 1994b). But the GOI did not realise the importance of a strong DoT at the time of privatisation. This led to large-scale antipathy towards privatisation from employees which hit morale. More than that, allegations of corruption weakened the case for reform in the mind of the public.

However, the GOI has realised the importance of the DoT in the post-privatisation era and is taking the necessary measures to strengthen it. As a first step, to face the challenges of privatisation, the DoT has formulated a perspective plan for 1997-2007. Apart from the strategies for meeting growth in demand, the plan includes the introduction of an Integrated Services Digital Network (ISDN) and intelligent network. The first one is a communications standard, which covers voice, data and image services up to all district headquarters by 2007. The second will include free local phone services and credit card billing in all the towns with a population above 0.5 million from 1997. The move towards ISDN[11] will be coupled with a fully digital network with all the electromechanical and analogue exchanges being replaced by digital ones. The plan also talks about the introduction of Personal Communication Services (PCS)[12] and a

Geographically Independent Numbering Scheme (GINS)[13]. The plan states that there will be extensive use of optical fibre in local, junction and long distance networks, with the replacement of all life-expired analog, coaxial and radio systems. The plan also calls for the provision of telephone connections to continue being provided practically on demand.

The GOI did not allow sufficient time for the preparation of the privatisation process and the absence of clarity in its intentions may well have acted as a disincentive to potential private investors. It attempted to attract investors by reducing bidding prices but the restrictions that it placed on the role of foreign investment in basic services operations may well have been counterproductive. Clearly the GOI felt that it was not able to make the investments in the sectors required and was not able to keep up with the rapidly changing technology in the sector. Nevertheless, it would appear that the Government was more concerned with the financial aspects of the privatisation process rather than raising levels of technological competence. The lack of transparency in the process of privatisation in the telecommunications sector in India has created confusion and doubts in the minds of both the public and employees of the enterprises affected (Arun and Nixson, 1988a).

Regulatory Experiences in the Telecommunications Sector

The essential purpose of any regulatory reform has been to transform the industry from a monopoly to a competitive market and to allow new services and technologies to enter and develop. Regulatory regimes must also take into account country-specific factors, political and legal as well as purely commercial. Regulatory practices may either fail or be less than effective due to the weak institutional capacity to enforce regulatory practices. There appears to be widening support for principles of regulation based on the criteria of independence, transparency and consultation, which will enhance the institutional capacity to enforce regulatory safeguards. In a significant study on regulatory reforms, OECD (1997) argued that:

1. Regulatory bodies should be structurally independent from any entity providing telecommunication services or equipment;
2. A regulatory body's rules and decisions should be transparent and broadly understood as a result of reasonably wide consultation;
3. An independent government body, not the telephone operator, should represent a government's position in international organisations.

In the pre-reform period, the policy framework in the telecommunications industry in India has been characterised by an absence of regulation. During this period, the monopoly service provider, DoT, formulated its own policy and set its own performance criteria reflecting public service nature of the service.

In 1996, the Government set up a statutory Telecom Regulatory Authority of India (TRAI). TRAI aims "to protect the interests of consumers, regulate telecommunications tariffs, settle disputes between service providers, ensure compliance of license conditions, bring about technical compatibility and inter-connections between different service providers, regulate arrangements amongst service providers in respect of sharing revenue, levy fees, facilitate competition, promote efficiency, provide a level playing field for fair competition among the public and private operators and to give further content to universal service obligation" (GOI, 1997, p.169). The Authority is expected to ensure transparency and accountability through transparent decision making processes, giving adequate opportunity to all affected before taking decisions, recording all decisions taken and subsequently publishing the same in an annual report. The TRAI has the power to seek information on all aspects of service provider's activities and to investigate any matter, which in its opinion constitutes public interest. The Authority also has power to inspect facilities, books and records of operators/service providers and to seek information, advice and inputs from any source it deems necessary.

The establishment of a regulatory agency was postponed until 1996 due to the resistance from DoT. Though it is quite reasonable that the DoT wants to maintain some control for strategic reasons, the fact that it is also a competitor in selected services questions its authority as a regulator at the same time. The basic purpose of regulation of public utilities is to optimise sector performance in terms of objectives set by the Government and to deliver the results in an impartial and transparent way. The role of regulatory safeguards in the transition to a competitive market is to prevent telecommunication operators with a privileged market position in infrastructure and services (like the existing state owned enterprise) from using the position to gain unfair market advantage in areas where the operator competes against other market entrants (OECD, 1997).

Several regulatory functions of the DoT exercised on behalf of the GOI have been divested to the TRAI, thus bringing its service-providing and tariff-seeking functions under the regulatory jurisdiction of an independent agency. The first petition brought before the TRAI was filed by Aircell Diglink (a joint venture between Sterling computers, Karthik

Financial and Swisscom) and other cellular operators against the unilateral order of DoT increasing tariffs for calls made from fixed phone lines to cellular phones (EIU, 1998). The TRAI struck down the order and rejected the DoT's subsequent appeal. But DoT is of the opinion that TRAI has no *locus-standi* on the licence agreement between the licence-holder and the former and complained that the TRAI has been too often interfering with its functioning which may bring down telecom sector growth in the future. Upset over DoT being dragged to TRAI, which in turn ruled against it, DoT went to the High Court, knowing full well that the Act allows the regulator to adjudicate such complaints in the public interest. But DoT argues that it has also been working in the public interest, and it should not be treated like an arbitrary body (The Economic Times, 27 January 1998).

The DoT contends that disputes between operators and the DoT on licensing matters (payment of fees, revocation of licenses) must be resolved according to the arbitration clause contained in the license agreement and not through the TRAI. However, there has been a growing realisation in DoT that most disputes have cropped up because of its mistake of making interconnect agreement as a part of the licence agreement (The Economic Times, 27 January 1998). Since most changes have been proposed in the interconnect agreement, a spate of legal disputes could have been avoided if the changes were carried out separately.

The jurisdictional tug of war between the DoT and the TRAI took a new twist in January 1998, with the latter writing to the Government expressing its unhappiness over DoT's move to sponsor amendments to the Telecom Regulatory Act which would dilute the compliance-enforcing power of the regulator. DoT argues that making any changes in the telecom license involves the licensor and the licensee, and TRAI has no role in that process. TRAI is of the opinion that the Act makes it incumbent to enforce compliance with the licence agreement by the licence-holder as well as the DoT and argued that any changes in the Act should be made in consultation with the TRAI.

Since the regulatory practises of the new environment are drastically different from the previous regime, there is a need for well-defined regulatory practices. To develop a more rational approach to economic regulation, the priority must be to establish a more coherent institutional framework (Ogus 1996, p. 341). Moreover, the potential benefits of privatisation are highly dependent on the effectiveness of the regulatory environment to meet the challenges during the transition from monopoly.

Conclusions

As experience with privatisation in the developing countries has broadened, it has become increasingly apparent that critical barriers to successful privatisation exist in the lack of suitable institutions and institutional capabilities to permit the privatisation process to go forward (Cowan, 1990). This is very much the case of India.

In India, till 1991 domestic manufacturers benefited from very high levels of protection from external competition and industrial production was characterised by entry-exit barriers in product and factor markets. The sustained period of ISI was associated with high levels of bureaucracy and associated problems of rent-seeking behaviour (Kaplinsky, 1997). Marathe (1986, p.14-15) observed the presence of strong regulation in the Indian economy during that period as:

> regulation took precedence over development....the regulatory momentum could not be checked.... A formidable and pervasive vested interest grew up in maintaining the system of regulation. The bureaucrat, the politician and, to some extent, sections of the industry which directly benefited from the protective consequences of the regulation constituted a combined lobby in favour of maintaining the system.

During this 'license raj', cost effectiveness of investment decisions received secondary status only. The thrust of the new policy is to remove the unnecessary and unwanted regulations which have been inhibiting efficiency and productivity. But occasionally the economic reforms may lead to the formation of special-interest groups that work for their own benefit within the context of the new policy. This is an important issue in India, because of the state's lack of autonomy vis-à-vis society. In this context, appropriate regulatory conditions are important to curtail the newly emerging interest groups.

The establishment of a coherent institutional framework for regulation requires proper allocation of functions to the regulatory institutions based on appropriate power and accountability, and this is a highly contentious issue. The major tasks to be performed by the regulatory institutions are two fold: (1) to establish the goals of a regime as an exercise of policy making and translating those goals into the principles and rules, and (2) procedures for explicating and enforcing the principles and rules and for the adjudication of disputes arising from them (Ogus,1996, p.99). The appropriate allocation of power to the regulatory institutions should contain both horizontal (the extent to which authority should be conferred on institutions other than the legislature or executive) and vertical (the degree of control exercised over such institutions) dimensions. The two main elements of independence - insulation from improper influences and measures to foster the development and application of technical expertise - are mutually supporting. But the experiences in the telecommunication sector reveal that, as in many countries, the GOI is reluctant to surrender political control over regulatory decisions.

The World Bank (1995) has ranked India among the countries that have been least successful in reforming their state enterprises, and argues that India met neither the desirability nor the feasibility conditions required for successful privatisation. India would have met the credibility condition in that it had significant domestic restraints on policy reversal and was regarded by investors as a relatively safe place to commit resources. Policy reversals to the detriment of investors have in fact been few, and the country has in general avoided broad macroeconomic imbalances. However, meeting this criterion alone is insufficient to overcome the inability to meet the desirability and feasibility criteria.

The concept of state owned assets were embedded in Indian society even in the period of Kautilya (278 BC). Arthasastra presents an illuminating picture of how public enterprises were conducting themselves successfully in that period. The importance of state owned assets was reinforced in Indian society at a later date by British rule and during the forty years of 'Nehruvian socialism' after Independence. It is natural to assume that ideological shifts take a long time to gain wider public acceptance. The impediments created by interest groups are not insurmountable if GOI is firm in its determination to increase private sector participation in development and has the necessary political will to push through the privatisation programme. How far and how fast the privatisation programme can and should be implemented depends on how policies are formulated in the broader perspective of economic, political and social realities of the country and relies largely on how GOI perceives its role in the reform process.

Notes

1   "The woods are lovely, dark and deep
    But I have promises to keep,
    And **miles to go** before I sleep".
    Lines from *Stopping by woods on a snowy evening* by Robert Frost (1874-1963). These words were found on a scrap of paper on the desk of first Indian Prime Minister Jawaharlal Nehru, at the time of his death.

2   The policy stated that - "After the initial exuberance of the public sector entering new areas of industrial and technical competence, a number of problems...[arose] Insufficient growth in productivity, poor project management, over-manning, and lack of continuous technological upgradation and inadequate attention to R&D and human resource development. In addition, public enterprises have shown a very low rate of return on the capital investment.... The result is that many of the public enterprises have become a burden rather than being an asset to the government (para 31).

3   The infrastructure sector includes services from public utilities (power, telecommunications, piped water supply, sanitation and sewerage, solid waste collection and disposal and piped gas), public works (roads and major dam and canal works for irrigation and drainage), and other transport sectors (urban and interurban railways, urban transport, ports and water ways and airports) (World Bank, 1994a, p.2)

4   The concurrent status means that both State and Central Governments will participate in the sector's development.

5   In terms of Section 59 of the Electricity (Supply) Act, 1948, SEBs are required to earn a minimum rate of return of 3 per cent on their net fixed assets in service, after providing for depreciation and interest charges.

6   It is an important indicator of operational efficiency of thermal power plants.

7   IPP projects can take different forms. Two structures are dominant-Build, Own and Operate (BOO) and Build, Operate and Transfer (BOT) models. The basic concern from the host country perspective is whether the structure has adequate incentives to ensure the necessary investor commitment and cost-effective operation. The concern from the investor's side is whether the situation provides adequate stability to own a facility for unbounded equity ownership (World Bank, 1996,p.7).

8   Orissa's power sector reform program has been prepared in consultation with the management, staff and labour unions of OSEB. Consultations with the public at large have taken place through the forum of the Orissa State Power Consultative Council, which brings together the State Government, OSEB and its main consumer groups. A comprehensive public campaign is also underway.

9   The Enron Development Corporation of Houston was the first foreign firm in India, after the reforms were introduced, with a proposal to set up a 2025 MW power plant costing $ 2.8 billion. The company was ready to agree to penalties for delay in construction as well as shortfalls in plant availability which were acceptable to the Government of Maharashtra and ended with a Power Purchase Agreement (PPA) between Dabhol Power Corporation (DPC) set up by the Enron and Maharashtra State Electricity Board (MSEB). Since the inception, a number of studies have argued that Enron enjoyed great leverage in the contract negotiations (as a pioneer in private power production in India) which would have resulted in heavy losses to the Maharashtra State Electricity Board due to the high cost of the power produced in the project. The new government of Maharashtra (1996) cancelled the project and renegotiated it with a price of $ 2.5 billion and reduced the agreed electricity rates by 25 per cent.

10   Although the NTP allows private participation in the basic telephone services, the private participants are required to maintain a balance in the coverage between urban and rural areas.

11   ISDN lines can carry data at higher speeds than normal analog lines and can accommodate several conversations at one time. The main feature of this concept is the support of a wide range of voice and non-voice applications in the same net work. The key element of service integration for an ISDN is the provision of a range of services using a limited set of connection types and multi purpose user network interface arrangements.

12 The PCS allows a subscriber to have one phone at work, at home and on the move, with different tariff structures depending on where the phone is used.
13 The GINS is a technology based on low orbiting satellites that allows a subscriber to have a global mobile phone with one number world wide.

References

Ambrose, W., Hennemeyer, P.R. and Chapon, J.P. (1990), 'Privatising Telecommunication Systems: Business Opportunities in Developing Countries', IFC Discussion Paper no. 10, The World Bank and IFC, Washington DC.

Arun, T.G. and Nixson, F.I. (1997), 'Privatisation and Foreign participation - The Indian experience', *Journal of the Asia Pacific Economy*, vol. 2, no. 2, 1997, pp. 201-224.

Arun, T.G. and Nixson, F.I. (1998a), 'The Transition of a Public sector monopoly: India's experience with Telecommunications', *Journal of International Development*, vol. 10, no. 3, John Wiley & Sons, Ltd.

Arun, T.G. and Nixson, F.I. (1998b), 'The Reform of the Power sector in India: 1991-1997', *Journal of International Development*, vol. 10, no. 4, John Wiley & Sons, Ltd.

Arun, T.G. and Nixson, F.I. (1999), 'Disinvestment of Public sector enterprises: The Indian Experience', *Oxford Development Studies* (forthcoming).

Bienen, H. and Waterbury J. (1989), 'The Political Economy of Privatisation in Developing Countries' in *World Development*, vol. 17, no. 5, pp. 617-632.

Bos, D. (1991), *Privatisation: A Theoretical Treatment*, Clarendon Press, Oxford.

Cook, P. and Kirkpatrick, C. (1988), 'Privatisation in Less Developed Countries: An Overview' in P. Cook and C. Kirkpatrick (eds.), *Privatisation in Less Developed Countries,* New York, Harvester Wheatsheaf.

Cowan, G.L. (1990), *Privatisation in the Developing World*, Praeger, New York.

Dutt, A.K. (1997), 'Uncertain Success: The Political Economy of Indian Economic Reform', *Journal of International Affairs*, vol. 51, no.1.

EIU (1998), *Foreign investment in India: Opportunities and obstacles*, The Economist Intelligence Unit, London.

Furubotn, E.G. and Pejovich, S. (1972), 'Property rights and economic theory: a survey of recent literature', *Journal of Economic Literature*, vol. 10, no.4.

GOI (1994a), *National Telecom Policy*, Government of India, 13-05-1994.

GOI (1994b), *Private Investment in Power sector: Myths and Realities*, Ministry of Power, Government of India.

GOI (1996), *Handbook of Industrial Policy and Statistics*, Ministry of Industry, Government of India.

GOI (1997), *Economic Survey 1996-97*, Ministry of Finance, Government of India.

GOI (1996-98), Disinvestment Commission Reports I-VIII, Ministry of Industry, Government of India.

GOI (1999), *Economic Survey 1998-99*, Ministry of Finance, Government of India.

Gouri, G. (1996), 'Privatisation and public sector enterprises in India: analysis of impact of a non-policy', *Economic and Political Weekly*, 30 November, M63-M74.

Kaplinsky, R. (1997), 'India's Industrial Development: An Interpretative Survey', *World Development*, vol. 25, no. 5, pp. 681-694.

Kautilya (278 BC), *Arthasastra*, Translated by Dr. R. Shamasastry, Wesleyan Mission Press, 1923.

Majumdar, K.S. and Ahuja, G. (1997), 'Privatisation: An Exegesis of Key Ideas' in *Economic and Political Weekly*, July 5: 1590-1595.

Marathe, S. (1986), *Regulation and Development India's Policy Experience of Controls over Industry*, Sage, New Delhi.

Mishra R.K., Nandagopal, R. and Lateef Syed Mohammed, A. (1993), 'Sale of public enterprise shares: frittering away the nation's wealth', *Economic and Political Weekly*, 27 Novenmebr, M 163-168.

OECD (1997), *The OECD report on Regulatory Reform, Vol.1 and 2*, Paris.

Ogus, A. (1996), *Regulation: Legal Form and Economic Theory*, Clarendon Law series, Oxford University Press.

Parikh, K. (1995), 'Enron episode: Lessons for power policy', *Economic and Political Weekly*, October 14-21, 1995.

Rondinelli, D.A (1995), 'Privatisation and economic transformation: The management challenge', in J. Prokopenko (ed.), *Management for Privatisation*, International labour office, Geneva.

Sanker, T.L., Mishra R.K. and Mohammed, L.S. (1994), 'Divestments in public enterprises: The Indian Experience', *International Journal of Public Sector Management*, vol. 7, no 2, pp. 69-88.

Vickers, J. and Yarrow, G. (1988), *Privatisation: An Economic Analysis*, Cambridge, MA: MIT Press.

World Bank (1992), Issues for Infrastructure Management in the 1990s, *World Bank Discussion papers*, 171.

World Bank (1993), Telecommunications - World Bank Experience and Strategy, *World Bank Discussion Papers*, 192.

World Bank (1994a), *World Development Report 1994*, Washington, DC: World Bank.

World Bank (1994b), Telecommunications Sector Reform in Asia - Towards a New Pragmatism, *World Bank Discussion papers*, 232.

World Bank (1995), *Bureaucrats in Business: The Economics and Politics of Government Ownership*, Oxford University Press for the World Bank.

World Bank (1996), Power Sector Reform in Developing Countries and the Role of the World Bank, *IEN Occasional Paper, no. 9*.

World Bank (1998), *Global Development Finance*, vol. I and II, Washington D.C.

6 Financing Global Environmental Protection in the Context of Indian Forestry

S P CHAKRAVARTY AND S R C REDDY

Introduction

Shared commitment for environmental protection has emerged as a contentious issue between the developed and developing countries (Barret 1994, Fairman and Ross 1996). The conventional wisdom is that the developed world has a greater stake in the long term benefits of environmental protection than the developing world, where the immediate need to increase consumption is paramount. Thus the poorer countries need external aid to encourage them to undertake conservation projects. External assistance – channelled through multi-lateral bodies such as the World Bank and bilateral agencies such as the British Overseas Development Agency – to India has accounted for almost half of the country's outlay in the forest sector in recent years. This assistance has been provided as long-term loans, subsidised interest rates, and direct grants. The following question arises: what fraction of the cost should be borne by India? If the problem is conceived as a game between donor countries and India, then it is in the interest of India to get as high a fraction of the cost as she can negotiate to be reimbursed by external sources. Likewise, it is in the interest of these external agencies to get away with as little as they can to persuade India to undertake conservation projects. It is argued here that this particular formulation of the bargaining problem is unlikely to produce much benefit to either side, and that the environmental issues in forestry require a different approach to articulating the idea of mutually beneficial international co-operation.

This article outlines the issues involved in developing environmentally friendly policies, and examines the structure of games between different actors. The rationale behind diplomatic games which entail richer countries compensating the poorer nations, if the latter nations undertake forest conservation and regeneration policies, is examined here. It is argued that these games need to take on board more forcefully the fact that it is also in the interest of developing countries to undertake environmental programmes.

The paper is organised as follows. Section I describes the role of forestry in the context of the greenhouse debate, and explains the part that forestry might play in this equation. Section II outlines the thinking behind diplomatic games as formulated in terms of enhancing alleged national interest. Section III points out the logical inconsistencies of the above approach to international negotiations. Section IV concludes with the argument that the diplomatic approaches to the problem of benefit sharing needs to be broadened to demonstrate that it is in the interest of developing countries to join in international efforts to reduce the impact of greenhouse gases. The case studies of developing countries discussed here refer to cases in India.

The Greenhouse Effect

Climate change and its economic and social impacts on global welfare have received widespread attention during the last decade (IPCC 1996). There is growing realisation amongst nations about the dangers of global warming, and there is increasing convergence of views about the need to arrest the emission of greenhouse gases which contribute to global warming. Among the greenhouse gases,[1] carbon dioxide has received much attention in international conferences on the environment. For example, European countries pledged unilaterally to reduce CO_2 emission at the last conference held in Kyoto.

Since carbon capture is a function of forests, the issues of conservation and regeneration of forests have assumed greater prominence in recent times. Conservation and regeneration of forests can reduce the emission of CO_2 into the outer layers of the atmosphere because forests act as a sink of carbon dioxide. One way of measuring the cost of damage is to estimate the impact of CO_2 emission on global output (Nordhaus 1991, Cline 1992, Fankhauser 1995). However, the scientific evidence does not allow for precise calculations of the benefits of carbon sequestration. Marginal environmental cost per tonne of carbon emission varies of $5 to $125, depending on the choice of discount rates and the structure of models used in these calculations. These are estimates at current levels of emission. Estimates of the marginal cost at the optimal level of emission can be obtained from models where the marginal cost of damage mitigation is set equal to the marginal value of the amount of damage avoided. Thus, estimates of marginal cost and marginal benefit coincide in these calculations, presented in Table 1 below.[2]

Cline (1992) uses a zero rate of discount to arrive at his numbers, but Nordhaus (1994), Peck and Tiesberg (1992), and Tol (1995) assume a pure time preference rate of 3 per cent per annum. An idea of the sensitivity of the cost estimates to the choice of the discount rate can be obtained by calculating the Fankhauser (1994) model for discount rates varying from 0 to 3 per cent. The marginal costs increase by a factor of 9, as the discount rate rises from 0 to 3 per cent. The following table provides estimates of the marginal cost of the reduction in CO_2 emission under the damage avoidance approach. The estimates of the marginal cost – US$ per tonne of Carbon abatement – are obtained for the optimal point, the level of emission at which the marginal costs and benefits are equal. The only exception is Cline (1992), where the figures represent the amount of global carbon tax, per tonne of Carbon emitted, needed to reach the optimal level.

Table 1 **Marginal Social Cost of CO_2 Emissions (US$ per tonne of Carbon)**

Study	1991-2000	2001-2010	2011-2020	2021-2030
Nordhaus 1993	5.3	6.8	8.6	10.0
Cline 1992	5.8	7.6	9.8	11.8
Peck and Teisberg 1992	10-12	12-14	14-18	18-22
Fankhauser 1995	20.3	22.8	25.3	27.8

The role of forestry in Carbon abatement programmes is undoubted, especially as a medium term measure for mitigating damages caused by carbon emission from industrial activity. These activities themselves will have to be addressed in the long term, but afforestation and forest conservation can provide mitigation now through carbon sequestration. Afforestation is a relatively cheaper option and action slowing the pace of deforestation is achievable at low cost to the world community. The potential for Carbon abatement through forestry programmes is outlined in Table 2 below. For the first row – the study by Sedjo and Solomon (1989) – the unit cost in US$ per tonne of Carbon sequestration is calculated here from the published figures in that study. A discount rate of 5 per cent is assumed with a rotation period of 40 years.

Table 2   Carbon Sequestration Potential of Afforestation Programmes

Study	Region	Afforestation Area (Mha)	Land Cost (US$/ha)	Treatment Cost (US$/ha)	Carbon Storage (t/ha)	Cost (US$/t)
Sedjo & Solomon (1989)	Global	465	400	400	6.24	7
Dixon et al (1991)	L. America	214	0	150-800	25-125	7
	Africa	222	0	30-1400		
	Asia	115	0	150-375		
Adams et al (1993)	USA	114	n/a	140-520	2.0-10.9	20-61
Price (1990)	UK		640	1640	2.09	96
Ravindranath & Somashekar (1994)	India	41.3	16	367-550	76-121	0.13-1.06
Xu (1994)	China	110.5	0	46-828	22-146	12
Masera et al (1994)	Mexico	18.2-19.6	0	387-700	25-150	5-11

The marginal abatement cost of CO_2 emission through forestry is between US$ 10-60 per tonne of carbon. If land costs are included, the cost rises to US$ 96 per tonne (Price 1990). The alternative, engineering measures, is considerably more expensive. The costs vary between US$ 100-250. There is also the consideration that the conservation technology – slowing down deforestation, promoting natural forest regeneration, and the implementation of global plantation and agroforestry programmes – is within the grasp of developing countries, especially if land costs are excluded and some external assistance is forthcoming.

Perception of Self Interest Amongst Nations

The benefits of conservation and regeneration of forests accrue widely, well beyond the frontiers of the country undertaking conservation measures. Also, the benefits of environmental programmes and costs of inaction are spread over time. Poorer countries may discount the future more sharply, concerned as they are more with the immediate problem of survival. The poorest amongst the poor may have a different agenda than the better off, even within a poor country. Thus the immediate perception of the need for conservation is not the same between countries. Finally the countries which undertake forestry conservation policies may not be the ones which benefit most. There is conflict amongst nations about the pace of CO2 abatement because countries engage in strategic behaviour when it comes to agreeing to their own share of contributions to the general global welfare. This tendency has been evident from the inception of the very first climate change convention (Escapa and Gutierrez 1998).

In the climate change debate, developing countries attribute the global warming problem to the energy intensive economies of richer nations. Governments of the developed countries are reluctant to accept this analysis, and instead they allude to deforestation and the inefficient land use practices prevalent in the developing world. The problem is this. If the industrialised countries are to address the problem of energy intensity, the structure of their economies will have to change. Transitional problems of unemployment and changes in consumption patterns provide a challenge for political leadership. Existing political institutions are ill equipped to cope with transition, and the rulers lack the imagination needed to grasp the nettle. The developing countries also have their own political compulsion. It is quicker to cut down forests to service international debts they have accumulated than to address the imbalance between government expenditure and revenue which may have caused the debt problem to develop in the first instance. Faced with the immediate need to maintain consumption, it is unattractive to pursue environmental projects which can yield economic benefits only in the long run. It is now accepted that some form of external assistance – eg, financial aid, interest rate subsidies, debt waiver, debt-for-nature swaps – is needed to encourage the developing countries to undertake conservation projects. It is the contention of this paper that it is not in the interest of developing nations to press for the maximum subsidy because the cells in the payoff matrix in the game between donors and recipients of subsidy cannot be precisely calculated.

During the last decade, several countries and also multilateral development institutions like the World Bank have provided assistance for investment in environmental protection. Between 1987 and 1994, 32 debt-for-nature swaps were negotiated in 15 countries, reducing their foreign debt by US$ 177 million and generating the equivalent of US$ 130 million in local currency for conservation.

For example, India has received assistance from the World Bank (WB), Swedish International Development Agency (SIDA), United States Agency for International Development (USAID), Canadian International Development Agency (CIDA), Danish International Development Agency (DANIDA), and the Overseas Development Administration of the British government (ODA). The data in the Table 3 are taken from a report issued by the Ministry of Environment and Forests of the Government of India (p.17, GOI 1989).

Table 3   External Assistance for Afforestation Projects in India in Recent Years

Indian State	Funding Agency	Project Period	Cost (Rs mn)	Target (ha)
Andhra Pradesh	CIDA	1983-90	383.78	150725
Bihar	SIDA	1985-91	538.57	168200
Gujarat	WB	1980-85	654	274280
Gujarat	WB/USAID	1985-90	1296.5	313400
Haryana	WB/DANIDA	1982-90	333.25	367000
Himachal Pradesh	WB/USAID	1985-90	572.9	112333
Jammu and Kashmir	WB/DANIDA	1982-90	237.4	44000
Karnataka	WB/ODA	1983-88	552.3	149500
Kerala	WB	1984-90	599.11	85300
Madhya Pradesh	USAID	1981-86	470	63450
Maharastra	USAID	1982-90	564	81000
Orissa	SIDA	1983-88	281.7	134400
Orissa	SIDA	1983-88	783.4	83500
Rajasthan	WB/USAID	1985-90	381.9	120800
Tamilnadu	SIDA	1981-88	591.38	224495
Tamilnadu	SIDA	1988-93	854	78380
Uttar Pradesh	WB	1979-84	400	95071
Uttar Pradesh	WB/USAID	1985-90	1611.6	161950
West Bengal	WB	1981-90	384.65	93000
Total			11464.44	2501284

The conceptual framework for apportioning the costs and benefits of environmentally friendly forestry projects is complex. Bargaining amongst countries for the share of the net gain from conservation has become a feature of life, but it is argued presently that it is not in the interest of any country to take a narrow view of self-interest. A pragmatic and co-operative approach would prove more fruitful.

Bargaining Amongst Nations

Suppose that a country undertakes a conservation project from which other countries also benefit. A globally optimal outcome entails that the aggregate costs and benefits – aggregated over all countries – must balance. To encourage the attainment of the optimal level of conservation, all countries may have to share in the cost of these projects. The remaining problem is to apportion the cost. This is not an easy task, but the problem becomes less intractable if it is formulated as a game amongst a limited number of countries. Generally the problem is viewed as a game between a developing country, which undertakes conservation projects, and the global community in the shape of the World Bank or one of the richer nations, bearing part of the cost of the project. If there is a Nash equilibrium which is also Pareto optimal, then the solution to this game is globally optimal. The literature proceeds along this line (Sandler 1993).

There is an insurmountable problem in arriving at a global optimum in a game as described above. The problem arises from the fact that neither player knows the benefit as perceived by the other player. The reason is that the benefits do not necessarily accrue immediately upon the completion of a project. Environmental benefits accrue to future generations as much as they do to the present generation. Political leaders who enter into negotiations about subsidies are handicapped by their immediate problems – for example, re-election prospects, and the need to secure higher levels of consumption now – from taking a long term view. The degree of handicap as perceived by a party is not known to the other party in these negotiations. Hence a poorer country may not correctly reveal the discount it places on future benefits, and a richer country may also dissimulate, to obtain advantage in negotiations. To appreciate the enormity of this problem, consider the following case of forest management.

It is reasonable to assume that the discount rate for India is greater than that by the richer nations on future benefits. The problem of increasing the level of consumption is more urgent and immediate in India. However, the precise degree of difference between India and a donor country cannot be known. Now consider the perceived carbon storage benefits by India and the Global Community of three projects. The first project is an afforestation programme with a 40-year harvest cycle. The second one is a programme with a 60-year harvest cycle. Both projects are in a forward looking regime, defined as a management regime in which investment in plant enrichment and new harvest is undertaken. The third and last project under consideration is a salvage-cum-plantation project, where the natural forest is consumed only to the extent that there is regeneration, and timber demand is met by new plantation.[3] Net gains to India and the Global Community can now be calculated under certain assumptions about the value of carbon sequestration. The payoffs are described in Table 4 below (Chapter 10, Reddy 1998).

Table 4 Payoffs to India and the Global Community (Rs mn/ha)

Management Strategy	India Discount Rate (% p.a.)		Global Community Discount Rate (% p.a.)	
	4	6	1	3
40-year harvest cycle	0.243	0.186	0.749	0.110
60-year harvest cycle	0.223	0.176	0.762	0.110
Salvage-cum-Plantation	0.274	0.136	0.921	0.151

In any negotiation based on sharing costs in proportion to the benefits derived, both parties may overstate their own discount rates resulting in a globally sub-optimal level of forest conservation. That problem may be partially countered by each side assuming that the other side is dissimulating by overstating its discount rate and making adjustments to the payoff matrix. However, the problem runs deeper. The direction of dissimulation cannot be known. It may well be that India would understate her discount rate, but the Global Community cannot know if India is understating or overstating her discount rate. This insight about the unpredictability of the direction of dissimulation was first explained in the context of the Coase theorem by Sarayadar (1983).[4]

To understand the paradox, suppose that the negotiation is about sharing the cost of a Salvage-cum-Plantation project as in Table 4. The true discount rate for India and the Global Community are 6 and 3 per cent respectively. Their net benefits are 136 and 151 thousand rupees, respectively. If India can get, as subsidy, half the difference between the above two figures, she obtains a payment of 7.5 thousand rupees per hectare. But suppose that she understates her discount rate – claiming that current consumption is less urgent – and takes the moral high ground over conservation. She may now be able to influence public opinion abroad in favour of a lower discount rate. The declared discount rate of the Global Community is forced down to 1 per cent. Then India can hope to obtain a subsidy of almost 324 thousand rupees per hectare. It may be clever to push for the maximum advantage in the bargaining game for subsidy, but it is not a wise strategy. India has done better in securing World Bank money set aside for forestry projects when the amount of money set aside for these has gone up (see Table 5), even if the share accruing to India has gone down. India would do well to raise environmental consciousness both at home and abroad as a means of increasing world-wide allocation for conservation.

Table 5 World Bank Lending to the Forest Sector in India and Asia (million US$)

Period	India	Asia	Indian Lending as % of Asia's Lending
1980-84	288	488	59.0
1985-90	347	957	36.3
1991-95	408	1760	23.2

Note: The 1991-95 figures include proposed lending. Source: World Bank 1992

Conclusions

Global warming poses a threat to both the rich and the poor. There are widely divergent estimates (see Table 6) of the impact of global warming, but the impact is smaller on the developing nations. However, as a percentage of the GDP, the impact is greater for the developing countries. What is important is to realise that the cost of global warming is significant for both the rich and poor nations alike.

Table 6 Impact of Global Warming on Developing and Industrialised Countries

Region	Fankhauser (1995)		Tol (1995)	
	Billion US$	% GDP	Billion US$	% GDP
OECD Countries	180.5	1.3	189.5	1.6
Rest of the World	89.1	1.6	126.2	2.7
World Total	269.6	1.4	315.7	1.9

Source: IPCC (1996)

Despite the fact that environmental protection is of benefit to all, and a co-operative solution is needed, recent international conventions in Rio and Kyoto about formulating a response to the growing problem of global warming have witnessed clashes between countries about who pays for conservation. These diplomatic wrangles are based on the assumption that governments represent the wishes of their people, and further that the wishes of the present generation adequately reflect the interests of those yet to be born. It is a barren approach and it is a recipe for inaction because the main problem is not confronted. Preservation of the environment entails costs which are not equally shared even within a country. There is scope for a country to influence the public opinion in another country. For example, a reduction in the energy intensity of consumption in the United States would be resisted by legislators sent to Congress by energy producing states. The political institutions in the United States cannot address the problem of internal distributive conflict. A similar problem arises also in the developing countries. Rulers in many developing countries find it expedient to service international debt by cutting down forests than by addressing the political priorities – inability to raise tax revenue, and unwillingness to reduce wasteful expenditure which may have given rise to the debts which now require servicing. They may have no policy to address the domestic problem of the trade-off between poverty and the environment (Reddy and Chakravarty 1999). Difficult internal problems can be side-stepped by concentrating exclusively on the problem of cost sharing between the developed and developing nations. There is a growing body of literature which attempts to formulate this dispute in terms of a bargaining model between the above two sets of countries. It is argued here that it is not in the interest of India, even if the object is solely to extract larger amounts of subsidies for conservation projects in forestry, to focus on the cost sharing problem. Instead, a concerted attempt by developing countries to raise environmental consciousness at home and abroad, which reduces the discount rate placed by political leaders in the richer nations on environmental benefits which accrue in the future, would be more beneficial to the developing world.

The exercise in consciousness raising would be more beneficial to poorer countries like India because global willingness to spend money on the environment would increase. If even a small share of this expenditure is captured by India as subsidy for afforestation projects, the total amount received could be larger than a large share of the small pool of money available in a world where there is no political will to spend money on environmental protection.

Notes

1. These are CO_2, CH_4, N_2O, CFC, and CF_4. Their global warming potential are discussed in publications emanating from the Intergovernmental Panel on Climate Change (IPCC 1996, Mabey et al 1997).

2. To avoid additional complications in measurement, secondary benefits are ignored. For example, prevention of tropical deforestation helps in the preservation of biodiversity, but this consideration is ignored. The aim is to get a plausible range.
3. The ideas of forward looking regime and salvage-cum-plantation are further explained in sections 9.8.3 and 9.8.4, respectively, in Reddy 1998.
4. The context is different in Sarayadar. He formulates the problem as a Coase bargaining game where the bargaining power between parties is not identical. Our discussion here sidesteps the difficult concept of bargaining power.

References

Adams R., Adams, D., Callaway J., Chang C. and McCarl B. (1993), 'Sequestering Carbon on Agricultural Land: Social Cost and Impacts on Timber Markets', *Contemporary Political Issues*, vol. 11, no.1, pp. 76-87.

Barret, S. (1994), 'Self-Enforcing International Environmental Agreements', *Oxford Economic Papers*, vol. 46, pp. 878-894.

Cline W.R. (1992), *The Economics of Global Warming*, Washington, D.C.: Institute for International Economics.

Dixon R., Winjum J. and Krakina, O. (1991), 'Afforestation and Forest Management Optionsand Their Costs at the Site Level', in IIED (eds), *Proceedings of the Technical Workshop to Explore Options for Global Forestry Management*, April 24-30, Bangkok, Thailand.

Escapa, M. and Gutierrez, M.J. (1997), 'Distribution of Potential Gains from International Environmental Agreements: The Case of the Greenhouse Effect', *Journal of Environmental Economics and Management*, vol. 33, pp. 1-16.

Fairman, D. and Ross, M. (1996), 'Old Fads, New Lessons: Learning from Economic Development Assistance', pp. 29-52, in Robert O. Keohane and Marc A. Levy (eds), *Institutions for Environmental Aid*, MIT Press, Cambridge, Mass.

Fankhauser, S. (1994), 'The Social Cost of Greenhouse Emissions: An Expected Value Approach', *Energy Journal*, vol. 15, no. 2, pp. 157-184.

Fankhauser, S. (1995), *Valuing Climate Change: Economics of Greenhouse*, London, Earthscan.

GOI (1989), *Report of the Working Group for Wasteland Development Sector in the Eighth Five Year Plan*, New Delhi: Ministry of Environment and Forests.

IPPC (1996), *Climate Change 1995 - Impacts, Adaptations and Mitigation of Climate Change: Scientific-Technical Analysis, Contributions of Working Group II to the Second Assessment Report of the Intergovernmental Panel on Climate Change*, Cambridge University Press, Cambridge.

Mabey, N., Hall, S., Smith, C. and Gupta, S. (1997), *Argument in the Greenhouse: The International Economics of Controlling Global Warming*, Routledge, London.

Masera, O., Bellon, M. and Segura, G. (1994), 'Forest Management Options for Sequestering Carbon in Mexico', *Biomass and Bioenergy*, vol. 8, no. 5, pp. 345-352.

Nordhaus, W. D. (1991), 'To Slow or Not to Slow: The Economics of the Greenhouse Effect', *The Economics Journal*, vol.101, pp. 920-937.

Peck, S.C. and Tiesberg, T.J. (1992), 'CETA: A Model for Carbon Emissions Trajectory Assessment', *Energy Journal*, vol. 13, no. 1, pp. 55-77.

Price, C. (1990), 'The Allowable Burn Effect: Does Carbon Fixing Offer a New Escape from the Bogey of Compound Interest?', *Forestry Chronicle*, pp. 572-577.

Ravindranath, N.H. and Somashekar, B.S. (1994), 'Potential and Economics of Forestry Options for Carbon Sequestration in India', *Biomass and Bioenergy*, vol. 8, no. 5, pp. 323-336.

Reddy, S.R.C. (1998), *User Group Benefit Appropriation in the Global Commons: An Economic Analysis of Tropical Forest Management under Uncertainty with a Case Study of India*, PhD thesis, University of Wales, Bangor (UK).

Reddy, S.R.C. and Chakravarty, S.P. (1999), 'Forest Dependence and Income Distribution in a Subsistence Economy: Evidence from India', World Development, vol. 27, no. 7, pp. 1141-1149.

Sandler, Todd (1993), 'A Tropical Deforestation: Markets and Market Failures', Land Economics, vol. 69, no. 3, August, pp. 225-233.

Sarayadar, Edward (1983), 'Bargaining Power, Dissimulation and the Coase Theorem', *Jounrnal of Institutional and Theoretical Economics*, vol. 139, pp. 599-611.

Sedjo R.A. and Solomon A.M. (1989), 'Climate and Forest', pp. 105-120 in N.J. Rosenberg, W.E. Easterling, P.R. Crosson, and J. Darmstadter (eds), *Greenhouse Warming: Abatement and Adaptation, RFF Proceedings*, Washington, D. C.: Resources for the Future.

Tol, R.S.J. (1995), 'The Damage Costs of Climate Change: Towards More Comprehensive Calculations', *Environmental and Resource Economics*, vol. 5, pp. 353-374.

World Bank (1992), Strategy for Forest Sector Development in Asia, World Bank Technical Paper 182, Asia Technical Department Series, World Bank, Washington, D. C.

Xu, D. (1994), 'The Potential for Reducing Atmospheric Carbon by Large Scale Afforestation in China and Related Cost/Benefit Analysis', *Biomass and Bioenergy*, vol. 8, no. 5, pp. 337-344.

PART IV
LABOUR MARKETS AND POVERTY

7 The Dynamics of Poverty: Occupational Mobility in Rural India

S PAL AND J KYNCH

Introduction

This paper analyses the nature and characteristics of occupational change and mobility among rural labourers in India. This is an important issue because it captures the dynamic characteristics of a poor occupational and social group.

Despite the facts that poverty is a very well-researched topic in India and that occupational mobility is important to an analysis of poverty, there have been few studies on occupational mobility. There are some studies on the related topic of income mobility. For example, using a panel survey of rural households carried out by the NCAER for 1968-70, Gaiha (1988b) finds that there are fluctuations in the economic conditions of rural households: out of the poor in 1968 about half ceased to be poor in 1970 while about one eighth became poorer. Out of the non-poor in 1968 about a quarter became poor in 1970.[1] These findings about rural households are similar to those from other non-Indian income mobility studies, which in summary show that, (1) there is considerable short-distance income mobility in poor households; (2) for many of the poor and not-so-poor, very low income may be a problem for relatively short, but ominously recurrent, episodes; (3) life-time income tends to be more egalitarian than annual income (Walker, 1995; Johnson, 1997).

Although income mobility captures some aspects of chronic poverty, Gaiha finds 'differences in the determining variables of the probability of being poor for households belonging to particular occupation groups' (Gaiha 1988a, 258). Furthermore, there is a range of problems associated specifically with agricultural households if income is used to measure poverty changes. Income variability within and across agricultural years makes the choice of time period critical. The reliability of income as a measure of rural standards of living is affected by flows of low value self-provisioning activities, the use of common property resources or rural access to public goods (Jodha, 1989; Bhattacharya and Chattopadhyay, 1989). There are also opportunities to smooth consumption patterns in the face of income fluctuations, and income is, therefore, a poor indicator of household expenditure or living standard (Dreze et al., 1992). Therefore, Drèze et al. (1992) argue that, in an agricultural economy with large fluctuations of income, current income is a poor indicator of a household's permanent income or economic status.[2]

In this study of one north Indian village over five decades, both income and occupational mobility are considered. The picture of economic mobility is rather different when occupational changes are used instead of income mobility. They conclude that, even in a village with 'substantial' current income mobility, the lack of occupational mobility among agricultural labourers is a profound influence on an association of that occupation and poverty.[3] Apart from this study, very little has been done so far to examine the implications of occupational mobility for rural poverty, at least within the economic literature.[4]

A point of departure of our investigation is that we concentrate on individuals' occupations within households. This has two advantages: first, that we recognise individual choice of employment, including different aspects of employment. For example, Sen (1975) emphasises that employment has income, production and recognition aspects, and these may be evaluated differently for individuals within the same household, which introduces the possibilities of discrimination or coercion, as well as intra-household bargaining. A second advantage is that we can investigate multi-occupational households, which may or may not be economically harmonious (Hunt, 1991).

One of the reasons for overlooking the implications of occupational mobility may be the lack of adequate data — in particular, information about changes in individual occupation over time tends to be sketchy (Vaidyanathan, 1989; van Schendel 1981). Nevertheless the importance of occupational mobility cannot be ignored because of its inherent dynamic nature. Using the data collected by the World Institute of Development Economics Research (WIDER) from six villages in West Bengal, we shall analyse the nature and characteristics of broad categories of occupational mobility[5] and the reasons for upward mobility of labourers.

The paper is developed as follows. Section 2 describes the occupational choice, change and mobility in the study villages. Section 3 provides the analytical arguments to rationalise the occupational dynamics. Subsequently in section 4, the change of occupation and upward occupational mobility are econometrically modelled and analysed for policy implications. The paper concludes with a brief summary of findings.

Occupational Choice and Change in the Study Villages

The WIDER Villages

A framework for analysis of occupational mobility in rural India has to take account of the particular regional or local context. The analysis in this paper is based upon the WIDER data from six villages in West Bengal for the period 1987-89. The study villages were drawn from different agroclimatic regions of West Bengal, four villages being in the south (Kuchly and Sahajapur in Birbhum district; Bhagabandasan in Medinipur district and Simtuni in Purulia) and two in the north (Kalmandasguri in Kooch Behar, Magurmari in Jalpaiguri). The villages of Kuchly, Sahajapur, Bhagabandasan and Simtuni were surveyed during 1987-88 and the northern Bengal villages of Kalmandasguri and Magurmari during 1988-89.[6] One distinguishing characteristic of the WIDER survey is that many of the social and economic data were based on complete enumeration of all households, the members being enumerated for information about educational attainment, earnings and employment experiences. In all, the survey covered 749 households and 3972 individuals. The survey's coding schema are used in profiling the villages and to describe the types of occupations and attempts to change jobs.

With respect to employment, individuals recalled information on their past and present occupations, and if they had tried to change their occupation in the past year. If they had not tried to change occupation, they were asked why not, and if they had succeeded in changing occupation, they were asked about conditions of employment such as migration, their work place (within or outside the village), employment status, wages and income, including any in kind.

These six villages drawn from different agro-climatic regions capture a good deal of the diversity present in rural West Bengal, exhibiting regional variations in demographic characteristics, educational achievements, income, poverty, employment, landholding and the impact of land reform (Table 1). This socio-economic diversity has been examined elsewhere (see Pal and Kynch, 1998; Sengupta and Gazdar, 1997; Chandrasekhar, 1993; Gazdar, 1992).

The inter-village diversity will be important to our analysis both because the particular environment influences dynamic aspects of individual and household employment, and because social relations are passed on to present generations. For example, in some villages (Bhandabagasan, Kuchli), agricultural developments such as use of groundwater and irrigation and seasonal leasing are associated with a weaker 'push' from agricultural to other employment; in other villages (Magurmari, Sahajapur) proximity to a local urban or industrial centre is associated with a higher proportion of income from non-farm activities. In all villages, landless households are usually tribal or scheduled caste. As we shall show, the occupational structure and ranking are sensitive to locally determined circumstances.

In terms of per capita income and the head count ratio, poverty is greater in the north Bengal villages, where wages are low, and in the dryland tribal village Simtuni in the south (Table 1)[7]. We shall examine if this view is maintained when we compare individual occupational mobility. First we shall outline village occupational structure and villagers' efforts to change their occupation, as recorded by the WIDER survey (sections 2.2

Table 1 Some Characteristics of the Study Villages

Variables	Kuchly	Sahajpur	Bhagaban -dasan	Simtuni	Kalman -dasguri	Magur -mari
Region	South	South	South	South	North	North
District	Birbhum	Birbhum	Medinipur	Purulia	Kochbehar	Jalpaiguri
No. of hhs.	142	227	134	75	89	49
Fsize	6.90	6.70	5.48	6.55	7.04	6.04
Landless hhs.	65	131	39	2	42	-
SC (%)	38	38	16	1	33	3
ST (%)	12	22	12	86	8	1
Muslim (%)	0	0	0	0	41	0
Literacy	0.38	0.40	0.66	0.10	0.52	0.35
[1]	(0.29)	(0.30)	(0.55)	(0.01)	(0.39)	(0.23)
Landreform	64	56	49	13	13	*
PNFINC	0.21	0.53	0.35	0.32	0.31	0.65
PCINC	1647	1545	2213	1160	1212	1441
Av. Daily wage	13.56	12.70	14.83	*[2]	7.66	10.92
HCR	40.4	52.3	16.5	62.5	72.7	56.6

Notes on variables: Fsize: family size; SC: scheduled castes; ST: scheduled tribes; Land reform: number of household who have gained from the land redistribution programme; PNFINC: proportion of income earned from non-farm activities; PCINC: mean income per head measured in rupees; Average daily wage refers to village-level mean daily wage earned from agricultural and non-agricultural work in 1988; Head count ratio (HCR): % of households below the poverty line.

[1]: Female literacy is in parenthesis. [2]: wages are paid fully in kind @ 5-6 kg paddy per da

and 2.3). We shall then consider some problems for our empirical analysis of occupational mobility in section 2.4. These are, first, the categorisation of occupations in agriculture; second, the ranking of occupations in order to indicate whether occupational mobility is upwards or downwards (rather than horizontal), including non-agricultural occupations; and third, how we take account of multi-occupational households.

Present Occupations

There is a problem of defining occupation in a society where individuals perform various remunerated activities. For example, an 'agricultural labourer' may also cultivate some land and perform other (sometimes seasonal) work, for example with bamboo or nut collection, small livestock or bidi-making. In the Indian research tradition, the problem is tackled by identifying a single primary occupation along with a number of secondary occupations reported by the particular individual concerned. WIDER researchers too adopted this distinction between primary and secondary occupations for each individual. Our analysis is based on the primary occupational categories identified by the WIDER.[8]

We first examine current primary occupations of the individuals in the study villages, based on cross-sectional data (see Gazdar, 1992; Chandrashekar, 1993). In general, agriculture is the mainstay of the economy in the south while non-agricultural activities seem to be relatively more significant in the northern villages, especially in Magurmari. Simtuni in the south is exceptional, suffering from a general lack of job prospects apart from regular migration.

Table 2 shows the recorded primary occupation of individuals in the study villages, and its pronounced inter-village variation. First, with respect to agricultural production, owner-cultivation is strikingly lower in Magurmari (north) and Sahajapur (south). Magurmari is close to - and a residential location for - the local centre and low paid work in, for example, arecanut processing and bidi-making. Sahajapur is near to the thriving district headquarter town. Second, the highest proportion of own-cultivators are in the dryland village Simtuni (49.5%), and green revolution village Bhagabandasan (38.8%). These two villages are at extremes of poverty and richness: Simtuni is a small village with almost no landlessness, but with extremely poor red laterite soil and dry conditions, while Bhagabandasan is a prosperous village which has developed agriculturally. Third, in all villages, attached labouring and tenancy are negligible as a primary occupation, in part due to Operation Barga.[9]

Turning now to unattached labouring and non-agricultural jobs, the distribution between agricultural and non-agricultural labouring is exceptional in Magurmari, where agricultural labouring is only 1.4 per cent against 42.5 per cent non-agricultural. The different employment structure in Magurmari is confirmed by the high proportion in trade and transport (32.1 per cent). Elsewhere, some non-agricultural jobs are also important: for example, in Kalmandasguri (labouring), Bhagabandasan (crafts, trade and transport) and Sahajapur (service).

Table 2   Occupational Choice in the Study Villages

Occupation	Village: percentage of individuals in each occupation					
	Kuchly	Sahajapur	Bhagaban-dasan	Simtuni	Magur-mari	Kalman-dasguri
Own-	35	18.9	38.8	49.5	11.3	34.5
cultivator	0.3	0.7	-	-	-	2.4
Tenant	50.8	46.6	30.2	37.3	1.4	30.3
Agri. labour	4.3	6.5	9.3	0.5	32.1	3.6
Trade etc.	1.8	4.3	11.2	0.5	4.7	1.2
Craftsman	5.2	11.9	6.2	2.8	4.7	4.8
Service	-	1.1	-	1.4	-	3.0
Attached lab	0.9	4.1	1.2	-	42.5	16.4
Non-ag. lab	-	0.7	-	-	-	-
Allied agri.	1.5	3.9	3.1	5.7	2.4	2.4
Professional	0.3	1.3	-	2.4	0.9	1.2
Others						

Except in Simtuni, individuals usually work within their village (between 77 per cent in Kalmandasguri and 95 per cent in Kuchly). Apart from working locally outside the villages, the prospects of successful migration are often not viable and even the existing opportunities are frequently seasonal (Rogaly, 1997; Breman, 1985). In the south, there is no migration in Bhagabandasan, 3 per cent in Kuchly and 7 per cent in Sahajapur; in the north, there is no migration in Magurmari and 1 per cent in Kalmandasguri. However, in Simtuni, 38 per cent work outside the village, and nearly half (47 per cent) of Simtuni's workers migrate (seasonally or annually) to the neighbouring districts. This constitutes a 'funnel' or known and predictable route to higher wage employment.[10]

Next we examine some aspects of occupational dynamics in the study villages. The discussion is divided in two parts: changes of occupation (section 2.3) and the nature of occupational changes (section 2.4).

Changes of Occupation

In this section, we consider the changes in jobs across primary occupations of each individual working member over a year. WIDER data contained two variables, namely, if the individual concerned has tried to change occupations (TRYCHNG = 1 if the person tried to change occupation and zero otherwise) and if s/he has succeeded in changing occupation (CHNGOCCP = 1 if the person was successful in changing occupation and zero otherwise). Four possible scenarios can be identified for different values of (TRYCHNG, CHNGOCCP) as shown in Table 3:

(0, 0) : individuals who did not try and did not change occupation;
(0, 1) : individuals who did not try, but changed occupation;
(1, 0) : individuals who did try to change occupation, but failed;
(1, 1) : individuals who did try and successfully changed occupation.

Table 3 Change of Occupation of all Household Members in the Study Villages

	Numbers of individuals (TRYCHNG, CHNGOCCP)				
VILLAGE	(0,0)	(0, 1)	(1,0)	(1,1)	Total
Kuchly	269 (177)	4 (1)	32 (10)	24 (9)	329 (197)
Sahajapur	387 (311)	3 (2)	32 (23)	39 (17)	461 (353)
Bhagabandn	189 (126)	1 (1)	51 (14)	17 (3)	258 (144)
Simtuni	198 (97)	1 (0)	6 (6)	8 (3)	212 (106)
Magurmari	167 (147)	3 (1)	19 (13)	23 (16)	212 (177)
Kalmandasgi	120 (70)	9 (5)	14 (9)	22 (6)	165 (90)

Note : Each entry denotes the number of individuals in each category. Numbers in the parentheses denote the corresponding numbers of those who were not cultivators in the past.

It is clear from Table 3 that in every study village, the great majority of individuals did not attempt to change their occupation. On further enquiry, two reasons were frequently offered as explanations. First, a significant proportion of individuals in all study villages (around 30 per cent or more) suggested that they were 'satisfied' with their present occupation, for example because there were 'mutual benefits' from staying with an employer. Second, between one-third and a half felt that there was a 'lack of opportunity' (except in Simtuni, where regular migration is established). If, as we might expect, 'satisfaction' with one's present job is inversely related to an expectation of success in seeking an alternative, which in turn is lower where there is a 'lack of opportunities', then prosperity would increase attempts to change jobs, even if many failed. In other words, a lack of alternative employment weights the risk factors.

This line of reasoning is partially supported by the discrepancy between the number of individuals who attempted to change occupation and the number who succeeded in the richer, southern agricultural villages

(Bhagabandasan, Kuchly). For example, in Bhagabandasan 68 tried but only 17 (25 per cent of the 68) succeeded, a high failure rate out of many trying. It is noticeable in the richer agricultural villages that it is cultivators who most often try and change occupation. By contrast, in the poor village of Kalmandasguri, few cultivators tried and failed relative to successes.

As well as those who tried and succeeded, a small number of individuals changed jobs without trying. Most of these were young (often the first time entrants in the job market) and in northern villages, and they moved into handicrafts or self-employment from cultivation. About half were from owner-cultivation.

Overall, the highest proportion of changes occurred in the northern villages and Sahajapur, in all of which the non-agricultural occupations have more importance. Thus, in Sahajapur 42 changed occupation and 71 tried to change occupation, in Kalmandasguri 31 succeeded and 36 tried, and in Magurmari 26 succeeded and 39 tried.

Nature of Occupational Changes

The nature of occupational changes depends on how we define occupational groups and how we rank them within an occupational structure in the village economies.

Van Schendel (1981) points out that occupational structure in agriculture is often argued to be 'too wide and unwieldy a concept' and that it is hard to know what constitutes upward and downward mobility. The rich complexity and dynamism of individual agricultural contracts in West Bengal is undeniable (Rogaly, 1996). Our purpose requires that we distinguish between broad occupational categories identified not only by the WIDER survey but also by other village surveys conducted in the state[11]. In particular, we have made use of the village surveys and resurveys conducted by the Agro-Economic Research Centre, Visva-Bharati (AERC, various),[12] the more recent work by AERC on modes of payment and conditions of employment (AERC, 1988), and Gazdar's (1992) analysis of inter-generational household occupational mobility in the WIDER villages. This body of empirical work suggests three distinct occupational categories for agriculturalists: owner-cultivator, agricultural labourer, and tenant or attached labourer. AERC (various) and Gazdar (1992) provide consistent supporting evidence for distinguishing two classes of agricultural occupations: owner-cultivators and agricultural labourers. The AERC reports emphasize first, that land is a desirable asset and therefore land-owning is desired (although working on the land is often disliked), and second, a persistent low status of agricultural labour ('the course of life of [a labourer in a landless family] is set in a narrow groove almost in a predetermined order', Mandal and Sengupta, 1962).[13] Gazdar (1992) points to the generationally persistent domination of social (caste) divisions of caste Hindu cultivator households and scheduled caste or tribal labourer households - there is, he remarks, 'stickiness around agricultural labour'. In addition to owner-cultivation and labouring, AERC (1988) proposes that sharecroppers and other non-wage, non-owner cultivators should be included as a type of labourer. We therefore take account of the diverse and versatile labouring contracts within three broad occupational categories, and, as outlined below, we include village level factors, or the villagers' reality as researched by the WIDER team, in order to refine how we rank them.

The ranking of occupations *within agriculture* is fairly straightforward: as remarked, land rights are important in West Bengal, and standard of living indicators (such as averaged income per household or per capita, expenditure per capita or consumption per capita) consistently rank owner-cultivators above agricultural labourers (AERC, various). However, Gazdar finds that, although generational mobility from owner-cultivator to agricultural labour households is usually associated with poverty, this is not true in resource-poor Simtuni. Therefore, in Simtuni, we rank migrant agricultural labourers above owner-cultivators.

Besides owner-cultivation, *self-employment* in crafts, trade and other agriculture-allied activities is usually ranked above labouring jobs in all the study villages. Table 4 suggests that the daily (imputed) wage rate in self-employment is comparable to that of owner cultivation or service jobs in

Table 4 Distribution of Daily Modal Wages in the Study Villages

Daily modalwage	Kuchly	Sahajapur	Bhagaban-dasan	Simtuni	Magur-mari	Kalman-dasguri
Own cult.	14.55	13.55	14.87	7	10	10
Self-emp.	14.55	13.55	24	-	-	10
Service	-	13.55	-	9	10	-
Agri.lab	14.5	12.7	14.88	9	8	10
	(13.56)	(12.93)	(14.53)	(14.3)	(9.8)	(10.14)
Non-agri.	11.7	5	-	2.26	10	12.8
labour	(11.68)	(11.96)	(-)	(4.15)	(6.9)	(11.06)

Note: These figures refer to the imputed daily wages. Number in the parenthesis refers to the corresponding average daily wage. '-' denotes missing value.

most of the study villages; but self-employment (like owner-cultivation) has added dignity attached to it, and rural households have a preference for self-employment rather than working for others (Walker and Ryan, 1990).

Service occupations are ranked above owner-cultivation: Gazdar's study (1992) of inter-generational occupational mobility of the household head suggests that in most cases in the six WIDER villages, a service occupation confirmed upward mobility in terms of land ownership and income rankings. Table 4 suggests that daily (imputed) wage rates for service jobs, in general, are higher than the labouring (agricultural and non-agricultural) jobs in all the study villages. In addition, the employment security aspect of these jobs was particularly attractive. In terms of individual mobility, many became teachers or were in other public sector, salaried work. In Simtuni, service occupations were often with the National Volunteer Force or Forest Department who employ scheduled tribe people.

The ranking of *non-agricultural labourers* is more complex, because sometimes an individual takes low-paid work through coercion or distress, and on other occasions the work offers an opportunity, for example in the proximity of an urban centre (Chandreshekar 1993). Chandreshekar argues that there has been little development of manufacturing in the villages. Therefore, whilst self-employment in trade and crafts offer upward mobility, other non-agricultural jobs such as labouring tend to rank more closely with agricultural labour. We have differentiated the rankings by using modal wage rates.[14] The modal village wages (see Table 4) rank casual agricultural labour above casual non-agricultural labour in the south (including Simtuni), and below in the north Bengal villages. Thus, a change from casual agricultural labour to casual non-agricultural labour would constitute a downward movement in the south, and vice versa in the north Bengal villages.

We shall now analyse the nature of inter-occupational changes over time, making use of our ranking of occupations. In particular, we shall focus our attention on former labourers (both agricultural and non-agricultural) who are identified to be the most vulnerable to poverty in most studies (see Drèze and Mukherjee, 1987; Drèze et al, 1992; also the village studies). We have disaggregated them into casual agricultural labourers, attached agricultural labourers or tenants, and casual non-agricultural labourers, and then examined how they have moved up or down the ladder in the recall period. Accordingly, one can distinguish between three types of occupational mobility: (1) zero mobility, (2) upward mobility and (3) downward mobility. The frequency distribution of former labourers among these three categories is shown in Table 5 in which each cell shows the number of labourers in a mobility category by village.

Zero mobility is the most likely event among former labourers in all the study villages. However, it is important for our investigation that the incidence of upward mobility is higher than that of downward mobility. Looking at the cases in detail, we observe: (1) in *Kuchly*, two casual agricultural labourers started self-employment in crafts and trade while one moved to a service job; there is no case of downward mobility. (2) in *Sahajapur*; seven casual agricultural and a non-agricultural labourer moved

Table 5   Upward and downward occupational mobility among former labourers

Village	Mobility		
	Upward	Downward	Zero
Kuchly	3	0	165 (96%)
Sahajapur	9	2	233 (94%)
Bhagabandasan	3	0	81 (96%)
Simtuni	1	2	79 (96%)
Magurmari	2	0	82 (98%)
Kalmandasguri	5	0	73 (92%)
All villages	23	4	713

Note : Numbers in parentheses refer to the corresponding percentages of the respective totals in the study villages.

to service and one agricultural labourer started self-employment. Two cases of downward mobility refer to casual agricultural labourers becoming attached agricultural labourers. (3) In the three cases of upward mobility in *Bhagabandasan*, two agricultural labourers started self-employment and another moved to service job. There was no case of downward mobility. (4) The single case of upward mobility in *Simtuni* was a casual agricultural labourer who moved to a service job. Cases of downward mobility were two casual agricultural labourers starting own-cultivation (ranked lower in Simtuni). (5) There was no downward mobility in *Magurmari*. Cases of upward mobility were two non-agricultural casual labourers starting self-employment in agricultural-allied activities. (6) There were five upwardly mobile casual agricultural labourers in *Kalmandasguri*; two started own cultivation, two self-employment and another one moved into service. There was no case of downward mobility.

Regarding inter-village variation of labourers' occupational mobility, we note that Simtuni has the least mobility of any kind, and northern Kalmandasguri has the most. Sahajapur is the village with greatest upward mobility; and these two extremes, Sahajapur and Simtuni, are the only two study villages with any downward mobility. The explanation is bound to differ; Simtuni has a general lack of opportunities while Sahajapur is evidently a more prosperous village, close to an urban centre. Indeed, within a more prosperous village, the downward mobility of an individual could be a more acceptable risk in multi-occupational households.

Many of the households in the villages are multi-occupational. However, occupational mobility rarely happened to members of the same household (two households of the 25 involved). Most mobile people are in households with other working members – only 7 of the 25 households had no other working member. In half (11) of the households of the upwardly mobile, at least one other member was a labourer. The possibility that the household allocation of labour (and therefore the nature of household decision-making) is a factor in mobility needs to enter our framework of analysis.

We have now shown that occupations can be ranked, and changes in occupations can be recorded and described. This part of our paper concludes that occupational structures differ between agro-economic regions, and with the proximity of urban centres. At a number of points in the description of occupational mobility (for example, the discrepancies between number trying and succeeding in changing occupation, individuals who changed without trying, or other household members' working patterns), the evidence suggests that individuals are constrained – or perhaps compelled – by local and household processes and characteristics, which will affect our analytical arguments.

Analytical Arguments

As already mentioned, issues of rural occupational mobility in developing countries have generally been undertheorised. We nevertheless need to specify the underlying theoretical arguments in order to rationalise econometric analyses of section 4.

Firstly we note that there is a huge literature on the functioning of labour markets, in general (Ashenfelter and Layard, 1986) and more particularly with reference to the functioning of the rural labour markets in developing countries (see Dreze and Mukherjee, 1987 for a survey of this literature).

In short, occupational mobility in traditional competitive analysis is a means by which labour supply adjusts to demand. As an extension of the basic competitive theory, human capital theory emphasizes that educated workers can command higher wages, and are likely to have a higher reservation wage than illiterate ones. A natural corollary is that poor people should invest in skills and other qualities in order to make gains from upward job mobility. There are also a number of extensions of the basic competitive theory with respect to imperfect markets and information; this literature has given rise to wide-ranging models like efficiency wages (Akerlof and Yellen, 1989), implicit contracts (Azariadis, 1975; Mukherjee and Ray, 1995) as well as models of disequilibrium labour markets (Malinvaud, 1977).

We are concerned especially with the rural labour market literature which focuses on labour contracts in which competitive conditions do not always apply, and where different wages obtain for the same labour: for example a 'village' wage (Rudra, 1982). Rural wages for a particular task often vary across sex, castes and between lean and peak seasons (Binswanger et al. 1984; Reddy, 1985). A distinction holds between casual (daily or piece-rated) and regular (attached or annual) labourers. It is well-established that daily regular wages are lower than that of daily casual wages (regular labourers being usually entitled to additional non-wage benefits). On the one hand, factors like farm size, irrigation facilities, cropping intensity or general agricultural development reflecting demand (Bardhan, 1984) and on the other hand, personal (age, sex etc.) as well as family characteristics (landholding, caste, occupation of the head of the household etc.) of individual labourers, reflecting labour supply considerations, determine the labourers' choice of contracts in the rural labour markets (e.g., see Pal, 1996, 1998).

As an alternative to the competitive theories, various forms of imperfect information models have been tested (see Dreze and Mukherjee, 1987). There has been some debate as to the applicability of efficiency wage models for rural labour markets (e.g., Dasgupta, 1993), but existing evidence tends to suggest the validity of implicit labour contract models, especially in the case of attached labour contracts in agricultural economies (Pal, 1998). One instrument which has received some attention in examining employment and rural well-being is the household bargaining model (Agarwal, 1994; Hunt, 1991). It is argued here that the possibility of individual choice of occupation will depend not only on the labour market, but also upon individual bargaining strength within the family and the associated family support (or lack of support) for individuated access to employment.

Arguments for Occupational Change and Mobility

In view of our discussion of rural labour markets in developing countries, we shall now examine the possible arguments for occupational mobility.

Let us start by considering a rational optimising individual. Any rational individual will choose to move from one job to another if and only if they can maximise the total expected gain (in terms of wage and non-wage benefits) over and above those of the previous job, net of all possible costs associated with this move.

Over and above the wage benefits, jobs usually carry various non-wage benefits such as working conditions, tenure, freedom and flexibility of work, provision of credit, bonuses and gifts or benefits in kind, which affect participation decisions. Individual valuation of non-wage benefits varies with personal characteristics of age, sex or disability, so that jobs have a subjective ranking, and individual mobility may be upwards, downwards, or neutral (i.e., vertical or horizontal).

Occupational mobility, whether vertical or horizontal, carries direct and indirect costs. Direct costs include costs of acquiring information, job search, and payments for licenses. Indirect costs due to changed domestic arrangements, changed social networks or psychological attachment to one's environment, may particularly affect older groups or young women with children. Casual contracts carry recurrent costs of job search, such as daily visits to a market place, which can be avoided if the employer 'calls' the employee. Migrant labour may be funnelled to one area or employer, reducing search costs. On the one hand, if an individual loses their job, their coerced mobility (vertical or horizontal) necessitates that these costs be met. On the other hand, a worker's decision to change jobs will take mobility costs into account.

Starting a different job (that is, making a vertical move) lowers initial productivity, especially in work where mechanical and ergonomic adaptation can be acquired, for example in manual labour like digging, or where on-job training takes place. This is a disincentive to take on 'less able' workers. Furthermore, it is a disincentive and burdensome to workers with poor nutritional or health status who will face higher energy use at first.

Implications for the Study Villages

It follows from our discussion so far in this section that workers' preferences feature prominently in their decision to try to change jobs (although we note the institutional context of preferences). One of the principal problems of unemployment and poverty in these predominantly seasonally agricultural villages is the lack of good and steady jobs throughout the year. A worker's decision to switch from one job to another does not necessarily mean that this is realised. The latter crucially depends on the demand for labour.

Assuming a given demand situation, our analysis primarily focuses on occupational choice, change and mobility from the workers' points of view while indirectly accounting for variation in demand through controlling job characteristics.   As argued earlier, an employee's decision to move from one occupation to another depends on a comparison of all possible costs and benefits in the new occupation over and above those of the previous one. These, in turn, depend on three sets of factors, namely, *personal* (e.g., age, sex, education, martial status), *household characteristics* (e.g., family size, family ownership of land and non-land resources, caste, family debt, if any) and *job characteristics* (wage and non-wage facilities, working hours, freedom and flexibility of work, work place within or around the village). On the one hand, for example, older people face disincentives to change jobs[15]; female members have less opportunity to get any employment outside the home which is perceived to be suitable by their family, and then to move from one job to another. On the other hand, educated members may have better opportunities for higher paid jobs in the village, or to migrate or commute to urban centres in search of a better-paid livelihood. Family land may act both as a constraint on full-time participation in the labour market and as a source of security for risk-takers. Given that the opportunity cost of time is higher for landed labourers, they may have less flexibility in market participation, job search or mobility.[16]

Many rural families are multi-enterprise, and individuals will bargain over how employment opportunities or job searches are to be allocated. Women who lack secure property rights or control over the product of their labour, are likely to be left out of this process. Members from families with large debts may be coerced into moving from one to another job; in some cases, however, indebted labourers may be constrained to work for the persons offering loan in the informal credit market.

Econometric Evidence

Our analysis of occupational dynamics in this section has two important aspects: we shall examine the factors determining (1) a change of occupation conditional on an attempt having been made (section 4.1) and (2) the likelihood of securing an upward occupational mobility among former agricultural and non-agricultural labourers (section 4.2).

Determinants of Change of Occupation

Let us first examine the factors that distinguish the successful individuals from among all the individuals attempting to change occupation. To this end, we shall use a bivariate probit model (see Greene, 1993) to jointly determine TRYCHNG and CHNGOCCP.

Suppose, Y_1 denotes if an effort was made to change the occupation (TRYCHNG) and Y_2 if the occupation was changed successfully (CHNGOCCP). The general specification for the bi-variate probit model would be:

$$Y_1^* = \beta_1'x_1 + \varepsilon_1 \text{ such that } Y_1 = 1 \text{ if } Y_1^* > 0 \text{ and zero otherwise}$$
$$Y_2^* = \beta_2'x_2 + \varepsilon_2 \text{ such that } Y_2 = 1 \text{ if } Y_2^* > 0 \text{ and zero otherwise}$$
$$E(\varepsilon_1) = E(\varepsilon_2) = 0$$
$$Var(\varepsilon_1) = Var(\varepsilon_2) = 1$$
$$Cov(\varepsilon_1, \varepsilon_2) = \rho$$

We use a maximum likelihood estimator to determine the model parameters, namely, β_1, β_2 and also the correlation coefficient ρ.

Using the arguments discussed in section 3, we assume that choice and change of occupation depend, for each individual, on personal characteristics, household characteristics (reflecting the supply of labour) and the job characteristics (reflecting demand for labour). To this end, we include three sets of explanatory variables reflecting (1) personal characteristics (AGE, SEX, MARRIED, PRIMSCH, SECSCH, HSECSCH), (2) household characteristics (FSIZE, HINDU, HEADCULT, HEADSELF, OWNLAND, SQLAND, DEBT) and (3) job characteristics (PASTCULT, PASTAGLB, OUTVILL) of individual members of the survey households (see Appendix for the list of explanatory variables). In order to control for the heterogeneous village characteristics (see discussion in section 1), we also use a number of village dummies (VILLAGE 1, VILLAGE 2, VILLAGE 3, VILLAGE 4, VILLAGE 5). Identifying variables in the two equations are DEBT, PASTCULT, PASTAGLB and OUTVILL. Mean and standard deviations of the explanatory variables are given in column 1 of Table 6. The maximum likelihood estimates obtained from the partial observability model are shown in column 2 of Table 6 (t-ratios are shown in parentheses). Results are summarised in Table 5.

These results confirm that family status pertaining to caste, landholding, and debt situation of the household, individual status pertaining to gender and schooling (to some extent, schooling is also correlated with family resources so that more educated individual usually belongs to a wealthier household) and job characteristics pertaining to the location of the job are significant determinants of (individual) occupational mobility in the study villages. The differences in factors determining the attempt to change occupation and those of the likelihood of being successful, points towards (1) the supply decisions in household economies and (2) also the constraint operating on demand.

Table 5 Bivariate Probit Estimates for Joint Determination of TRYCHNG and CHNGOCCP for All Households

Variables	(1) Mean (s.d.)	(2) TRYCHNG	CHNGOCCP
ONE	-	-0.45 (2.309)*	-1.35 (4.802)**
AGE	35.42 (12.63)	-0.006 (1.774)*	0.004 (1.956)*
SEX	0.46 (0.50)	-0.86 (5.169)**	-0.57 (2.559)*
MARRIED	0.78 (0.42)	-0.003 (0.029)	0.01 (0.068)
PRIMSCH	0.17 (0.37)	-0.09 (0.774)	0.17 (1.272)
SECSCH	0.20 (0.40)	0.36 (3.416)**	0.43 (3.440)**
HSECSCH	0.04 (0.19)	0.92 (3.411)**	0.37 (0.986)
FSIZE	5.97 (2.94)	-0.007 (0.456)	-0.02 (1.122)
HEADCULT	0.32 (0.47)	-0.24 (1.912)*	-0.23 (1.532)
HEADSELF	0.15 (0.36)	0.02 (0.180)	0.08 (0.592)
HINDU	0.34 (0.0.30)	-0.31 (3.199)**	-0.08 (0.643)
DEBT	0.6 (0.62)	-	0.21 (2.350)*
OWNLAND	1.74 (2.82)	0.10 (2.259)*	0.09 (1.966)*
SQLAND	10.98 (33.33)	-0.006 (1.973)*	-0.005 (1.515)
PASTCULT	0.87 (0.34)	0.13 (1.307)	-
PASTAGLB	0.04 (0.19)	-0.007 (0.040)	-
OUTVILL	0.16 ( )	-	0.45 (3.971)**
VILLAGE1	0.20 (0.40)	-0.21 (1.356)	-0.53 (2.765)*
VILLAGE2	0.28 (0.45)	0.39 (1.900)*	-0.17 (0.636)
VILLAGE3	0.16 (0.36)	-0.03 (0.166)	-0.64 (3.173)**
VILLAGE4	0.13 (0.34)	-0.76 (3.531)**	-1.22 (4.356)**
VILLAGE5	0.13 (0.34)	-0.04 (0.208)	-0.33 (1.752)
Rho(1,2)	-	0.86 (32.777)**	
Log-likelihood	-	-946.5349	
No. of obs.	1637	1637	

Note : '*' denotes that the variable concerned is significant at least at 10% and '**' denotes the same at 1% level of significance.

Determinants of TRYCHNG (Y_1)

(1)   Younger individuals are more likely to try changing occupations than the older ones.

(2)   Male members of the household are more likely to try changing occupation.

(3)   Individuals with secondary and higher secondary schooling are more likely to attempt to change occupation.

(4)   Individuals from families with higher caste (Hindus), and with the head of the household in owner cultivation are *less* likely to try to change occupation. However, individuals from families with larger landholding are *more* likely to try to change occupation.

Determinants of CHNGOCCP (Y_2)

(1)   Among those who tried to change occupation, relatively older individuals are more likely to be successful in changing occupation.

(2)   Male members of the household have significantly greater likelihood of successfully changing occupation.

(3)   Individual members with secondary schooling are more likely to be successful (coefficient of higher secondary schooling, however, is not significant).

(4)   Family characteristics too play a significant role, though the effect is different from that of TRYCHNG. Individuals from families with larger landholding and higher debt are more likely to succeed in changing occupation in the study villages: while the former reflects the social status and economic security, the latter reflects the motivation to change for the better.

Determinants of Occupational Mobility Among Labourers

Secondly, we examine the factors determining the nature of occupational mobility. To this end, we focus on the casual and attached agricultural and casual non-agricultural labourers of the past (as discussed in section 2). Since the incidence of downward mobility was small among the labourers in the study villages, we consider the nature and characteristics of upward mobility among labourers (after discarding four cases of downward mobility). We define the variable UPWARD as follows:

$$\text{UPWARD} = 1 \text{ if upward mobility}$$
$$= 0 \text{ if zero mobility}$$

Assuming that a set of explanatory variables x determines the poverty status, the following relation holds good.

$$\text{Prob[UPWARD} = 1] = F(x, \delta)$$
$$\text{Prob[UPWARD} = 0] = 1 - F(x, \delta)$$

where F is the cumulative distribution function and δ is the set of parameters to be estimated. The parameter vector δ reflects the impact of changes in any of the x's on the probability that UPWARD = 1. In this regard, one can use any continuous distribution; in practice, however, the use of a probit model which uses a normal distribution is common (Maddala, 1983; Greene, 1991).

In view of our discussion of section 3, we use similar explanatory variables as in section 3.1. For example, we include the same set of personal characteristics (AGE, SQAGE, SEX, MARRIED, PRIMSCH, SECSCH). So far as household characteristics are concerned, we consider different occupations of head of the household (HEADCULT, HEADSELF, HEADSERV), different castes (HINDU, SC, ST). Among job characteristics, we now include two variables, namely, SATISFD (if the individual concerned is satisfied with the present occupation) and OUTVILL (if the individual concerned works outside the village as a non-migrant). As before, five village dummies (VILLAGE 1, VILLAGE 2, VILLAGE 3, VILLAGE 4, VILLAGE 5) are included to account for the variation in various village characteristics which have not been included.

The parameter vector δ is estimated by maximising the probit log-likelihood function (see Greene, 1993).[17] These estimates are shown in Table 7 (t-ratios are shown in the parentheses).

(1)   Personal characteristics like age and gender are significant. Age tends to enhance the likelihood of securing an upward mobility. However, the coefficient of square of age is negatively significant, suggesting that the likelihood of an upward mobility increases with age, but at a decreasing rate. The coefficient of the gender dummy implies that male labourers are more likely to experience upward mobility. Both primary and secondary education help movement up the occupational ladder, even among agricultural labourers.

(2)   Family background of an individual labourer appears to be highly significant; in particular, occupation of the head of the household and the family landholding play an important role though none of the caste variables is significant. Individual members from households with larger land holdings are more likely to experience upward occupational mobility. Moreover, the likelihood of securing upward mobility is higher if the head of the household is an owner-cultivator,

self-employed or service holder, but not if the head is an agricultural labourer.

(3)   Finally we observe that job characteristics are also important. For example, the likelihood of securing upward mobility appears to be higher if the individual is working outside the village, but lower if s/he is satisfied with the present work.

Table 7   Maxmimum Likelihood Probit Estimates of Upward Occupational Mobility

Variables	Mean (s.d.)	Occupational Mobility Upward
ONE	-	-6.59 (3.742)**
AGE	33.93 (11.89)	0.15 (1.708)*
SQAGE	1292.32 (917.73)	-0.002 (1.680)*
SEX	0.52 (0.5)	-0.76 (1.683)*
MARRIED	0.77 (0.42)	0.70 (1.457)
PRIMSCH	0.16 (0.37)	0.93 (2.800)**
SECSCH	0.13 (0.33)	1.19 (1.971)*
OUTVILL	0.16 (0.37)	0.84 (2.161)*
SATISFD	0.43 (0.5)	-0.99 (2.912)**
HEADCULT	0.09 (0.3)	0.85 (1.758)*
HEADSELF	0.20 (0.4)	2.09 (5.119)**
HEADSERV	0.04 (0.21)	1.43 (3.010)**
HEADAGLB	0.48 (0.5)	0.10 (0.187)
HINDU	0.08 (0.84)	-0.44 (0.461)
SC	0.47 (0.50)	0.78 (1.107)
ST	0.38 (0.49)	0.91 (1.292)
DEBT	1.47 (0.54)	0.09 (0.359)
OWNLAND	0.67 (1.57)	0.46 (2.312)*
VILLAGE 1	0.18 (0.39)	-0.41 (0.761)
VILLAGE 2	0.33 (0.47)	0.70 (1.028)
VILLAGE 3	0.14 (0.34)	-0.37 (0.572)
VILLAGE 4	0.09 (0.3)	-2.5 (2.377)*
VILLAGE 5	0.17 (0.37)	-0.88 (1.197)
Log-likelihood	-	-60.4067
Chi-square	-	110.0736**
No. of obs.	728	728

Note : '*' denotes that the variable concerned is significant at least at 10% and '**' denotes the same at 1% level of significance.

Marginal Effects of Family Landholding and Schooling on Occupational Mobility

The dependent variable of a probit model is discrete in nature; hence, the probit estimates do not reflect the marginal effects of the explanatory variables. That is why we shall now calculate the marginal effects of change in (1) landholding and (2) primary schooling on the prospect of securing an upward mobility at the mean vectors of other explanatory variables for male and female married labourers, working in the village from scheduled caste households where the head is an owner cultivator as follows:

$$\frac{\partial(\text{UPWARD})}{\partial_{xj}} = \phi(\beta'_{xj})\beta_j$$

where ϕ is the standard normal density. In particular, we calculate these predicted probabilities for individuals with (1) average village-level landholding (0.19, 0.09, 0.18, 2.4 and 0.08 respectively in the five villages as shown in tables 8, 9) and also (2) maximum village-level landholding (1.7, 1.72, 1.89, 8.27, 2.05 acres for these five villages respectively as shown in Tables 8 and 9) with and without primary schooling. These estimates are shown in Table 8.

Our main observations from the calculation of marginal effects on upward mobility of an increase in the family landholding (see Table 8) are as follows:

(1)   The marginal effect of an increase in the family landholding is consistently higher for a male labourer in all the study villages.
(2)   For a given sex, the marginal effect is higher if the individual concerned has primary schooling.
(3)   For a given sex, the marginal effect on the probability of upward mobility is higher if the individual concerned comes from a family with higher landholding (see column 3 and 4).
(4)   The effect of larger family landholding is even bigger if the individual concerned has primary schooling than for those without (compare column 1 & 2 with 3 & 4).
(5)   An intervillage comparison of these marginal effects suggests that the prospect of upward mobility is the highest in the south Bengal village of Sahajapur, situated near a prosperous town centre. In comparison, the prospect is considerably lower in Simtuni in Purulia and Magurmari in Jalpaiguri. Simtuni has few job opportunities in the village. Average landholding (2.4 acres) is

much higher in the village compared to the other study villages, but the land quality is poor and it is situated in the dryland area of Purulia.

Table 8 Marginal effects of landholding on the probability of securing upward occupational mobility

		Kuchly	Sahajpur	Villages Bhagaban	Simtuni	Magurmari
Mean land & no primary school (1)	Male	0.02	0.12	0.02	0.001	0.006
	Female	0.004	0.04	0.003	0.0001	0.0006
Mean land with primary school (2)	Male	0.09	0.18	0.09	0.01	0.04
	Female	0.03	0.13	0.03	0.002	0.009
Max. land & no primary school (3)	Male	0.07	0.18	0.07	0.08	0.04
	Female	0.02	0.12	0.02	0.02	0.01
Max. land with primary school (4)	Male	0.17	0.14	0.17	0.17	0.13
	Female	0.09	0.18	0.09	0.08	0.05

Next we calculate the marginal effects of primary schooling as shown in Table 9. Similar inferences to those derived from Table 8 still hold good. More interestingly, we can now compare the marginal effects of family landholding and those of primary schooling. It clearly follows that other things remaining unchanged, marginal effects on upward occupational mobility are higher from a marginal increase in primary schooling than those from a marginal increase in family landholding.

Table 9   Marginal effects of Primary Schooling on occupational mobility

		Villages				
		Kuchly	Sahaipu	Bhagab	Simtuni	Magur
Mean land & no primary school	Male	0.04	0.24	0.04	0.002	0.01
	Female	0.007	0.09	0.006	0.0002	0.001
Mean land with primary school	Male	0.20	0.37	0.18	0.03	0.09
	Female	0.06	0.27	0.05	0.004	0.02
Max. land & no primary school	Male	0.15	0.36	0.15	0.03	0.08
	Female	0.04	0.23	0.04	0.17	0.02
Max. land with primary school	Male	0.34	0.29	0.34	0.17	0.27
	Female	0.18	0.37	0.19	0.35	0.11

	Marginal effects of family landholding				Marginal effects of primary schooling			
	Mean land & no primary school		Mean land with primary school		Mean land & no primary school		Mean land with primary school	
	Male	Female	Male	Female	Male	Female	Male	Female
Simtuni	0.01	0.002	0.07	0.02	0.02	0.003	0.14	0.03

Finally we focus on Simtuni where the prospect of upward occupational mobility is bleak for the labourers who are *working in the village* (see Tables 8 and 9). That is why we consider the labourers *working outside the village* and allow them to have an additional unit of family landholding and primary schooling. The corresponding marginal effects are shown on page 125.

Marginal effects of both landholding and primary schooling increase while the latter are still higher than the former - again emphasising the sheer lack of employment opportunities in this village.

Concluding Remarks

The paper was motivated by the dearth of economic analyses of occupational mobility among agricultural labourers who are the group most vulnerable to poverty. In view of the difficulties of defining occupation in a rural context, the first step of our analysis was to identify the broad categories of occupations between which vertical mobility takes place. Obviously any analysis of the nature of occupational mobility is dependent on the ranking of occupations in these village economies. Having investigated the problems, our decisions were based upon empirical investigations, especially those of AERC and the WIDER surveys in West Bengal. We ranked individual member's primary occupation accordingly, considering both wage and non-wage criteria. Secondly, we have analysed the factors (1) causing a change of occupation among the labourers who tried to change occupation over a twelve-month recall period and (2) enhancing the prospect of upward mobility, examining data from six villages in West Bengal which exemplify regional diversity, different levels of prosperity, and different patterns of employment between agricultural and non-agricultural activities.

Our analysis focused on occupational dynamics of the individual labourers. We noted the discrepancy between the numbers of labourers who try to change occupation and the number who succeed, and that the difference primarily reflects the lack of demand for labour. Being young or having schooling experience positively affects the probability of trying to change occupation, but not the probability of success. Success is more dependent upon socially constructed 'status' – being older, male or from larger farming families.

We then analysed the nature of occupational mobility: upwards, downwards or zero mobility among both agricultural and non-agricultural labourers. Neutral mobility (including no change) is most common, as has been observed in other studies. Probit analysis of upward occupational mobility among labourers suggests that the prospect of upward mobility increases with individual age and schooling; being female lowers the probability of upward mobility. The prospect of upward mobility is significantly higher if the individual comes from a family with a large landholding and decreases if the individual is 'satisfied' with their occupation. There are also disadvantages of being in an agricultural labouring household as opposed to a household where the head is an owner-cultivator, self-employed or is engaged in a service job, and the advantages of working outside the village (as a non-migrant).

Despite some (surmountable) difficulties of defining and ranking occupations, analysis of occupational mobility has obvious significance for the analysis of poverty among agricultural labourers, in particular because it captures both the possibilities of individual choice in a multi-occupational household and the problems of constraints in a dynamic way. The concept of occupational mobility also encapsulates various static poverty indicators such as landholding and education within a composite measure, and we explored their complementarity with occupational mobility as possible policy instruments. A long-term policy to reduce chronic poverty in rural India needs to address the opening of occupational choice to the agricultural labourers.

Notes

1. Considering the poor in 1968 who moved up in 1970, Gaiha argued that to a large extent this can be attributed to access to more land and to the use of modern inputs in production which was initiated by the introduction of new technology.
2. The study over 5 decades of one village (Dreze et al 1992; see especially Lanjouw and Stern (1998) is unique in that longitudinal data makes the it possible to compare current or permanent income and occupational changes.
3. The strong association of agricultural labour with poverty is compounded by their lack of mobility out of that occupation and out of poverty' (Lanjouw and Stern, 1998:370).
4. Gazdar (1992) examines the nature of inter-generational mobility for household heads in six villages in West Bengal and observed considerable stickiness around agricultural labour. There is, of course, sociological and anthropological literature which includes many insights into occupational mobility but within a different perspective from that of this paper: for example, Shanin (1972), van Schendel (1981), Rahman (1986). Among other studies of rural India and Bangladesh from which an investigation of occupational mobility can be enriched, see also Bliss and Stern (1982), Dreze et al. (1992), Bardhan (1989), Agarwal (1986), Indra and Buchignani (1997), Rogaly (1996, 1997), Breman (1985), Jodha (1989, 1994).
5. The words occupational mobility and job mobility are used synonymously in the paper.
6. Sen and Sengupta (1983) report on an earlier nutritional survey of two of these villages (Kuchly and Sahajapur) in January-April 1983. In addition, the literature on

the villages from the UNU/WIDER project 1987-89 includes Sengupta and Gazdar (1997), Chandrasekhar (1993), Gazdar (1992).

7. The low literacy in Simtuni is striking. Using the Census 1991 data, Sengupta and Gazdar (1997) contrast the literacy rates among different castes in rural West Bengal; while the literacy rate is 82% for caste Hindu, it is as low as 15% for scheduled tribes and even smaller for female members of these lowest caste households.

8. In view of the complexity of the occupational structure, some may argue that the occupational categories defined in the WIDER data-set are rather broad. Our purpose is to examine vertical mobility rather than horizontal mobility, and the categorisation shows significant number of individuals moving between occupations and, therefore, enables us to investigate the occupational dynamics in an effective way. The rich complexity of rural labour contracts in West Bengal is explored in Rogaly (1997).

9. This was the legislative operation introduced by the West Bengal government in the late 70s to ensure the security in land for the tenant farmers (who are called bargadars in the region).

10. This can result in 'clusters' of employees in a particular locality or with one employer.

11. Given the difficulties of ranking occupation, this enables us to capture the villager's perception of the nature of occupational mobility which is very important for our analysis.

12. These took place between 1956 and 1968, and the reports that we consulted are on villages in the following districts: Birbhum (including Sahajapur, which may now have research fatigue), Santhal Parganas, Durgapur, Medinipur, Koch Behar, Howrah, Bankura, Burdwan and 24 Parganas, reported in the series *Studies in Rural Change*.

13. The AERC survey reports were based on a division into primary and secondary occupation, and categorised individuals as self-supporting, earning dependent and dependent.

14. Daily average wages of agricultural and non-agricultural labourers in the study villages is given in Gazdar (1992: 50).

15. It can be argued that older people will have less working life left to make up for the mobility costs incurred which, in turn, suggests that their time preferences and discount factors are higher, and their value of future gains lower when compared to younger people, which would reduce mobility of older people.

16. There is a close relationship between the ownership of land and non-land resources and the caste of the family: very often larger farms are also the owners of more non-land resources and they belong to higher castes as well. Also, one needs to identify the close correspondence between the distribution of household resources and that of individual schooling in these rural household economies. These factors will be further discussed while interpreting our results.

17. Given that only a small proportion of labourers are mobile in the sample, there may arise hazards in modelling upward mobility using standard probit model; often robustness is a problem. However, it is evident from the t-ratios in Table 6 that a number of explanatory variables are highly statistically significant (and they have been systematically significant in various alternative specifications that we tried), irrespective of the low frequency of non-zero cases, thus allowing us to analyse these important issues further.

Appendix

List of regression variables

I. Individual Characteristics
AGE : Age in years
SQAGE : Square of age
SEX : 1 for female and zero for male
MARRIED : 1 for married members and zero otherwise
SCHOOL : 0 for illiterate, 1 for primary school, 2 for secondary school, 3 for others.
ILLIT : 1 if illiterate and zero otherwise
PRIMSCH : 1 if with primary schooling and zero otherwise
SECSCH : 1 if with secondary schooling and zero otherwise
HSECSCH : 1 if with secondary schooling and zero otherwise
INVILL : 1 if working in the village and zero otherwise
OUTVILL : 1 if working outside the village and zero otherwise
NOOP : 1 if the individual thinks that there is no opportunity for changing occupation
SATSFD : 1 if the individual was satisfied with the job and zero otherwise
PASTCULT : 1 if the individual was an owner cultivator previously and zero otherwise
PASTAGLB : 1 if the individual was an agricultural labourer previously and zero otherwise
NOWCULT : 1 if the individual is an owner cultivator at present and zero otherwise
NOWAGLB : 1 if the individual is an agricultural labourer at present and zero otherwise.

II. Household Characteristics
FSIZE : Number of family members
HEADCULT : 1 if the Head of the household is an owner cultivator at present and zero otherwise
HEADAGLB : 1 if the Head of the household is an agricultural labourer at present and zero otherwise
HEADSELF : 1 if the Head of the household is self-employed at present and zero otherwise
CASTE : 1 for Hindu, 2 for scheduled caste, 3 for scheduled tribe and 4 for Muslim
HINDU : 1 if Hindu and zero otherwise
SC : 1 if scheduled caste and zero otherwise
ST : 1 if scheduled tribe and zero otherwise
DEBT : 1 if the family has some debt to repay and zero otherwise
OWNLAND : Size of family landholding in acres.

III. Village Characteristics
VILLAGE 1 : Kuchly
VILLAGE 2 : Sahajapur
VILLAGE 3 : Bhagabandasan
VILLAGE 4 : Simtuni
VILLAGE 5 : Magurmari.

References

AERC (1988), 'Employment conditions and modes of wage payments of agricultural labour in Birbhum, West Bengal', Agro-Economic Research Centre, Visva-Bharati, Santiniketan.

AERC (various), *Studies in Rural Change*, Reports on surveys and re-surveys of villages in West Bengal, Agro-Economic Research Centre, Visva-Bharati, Santiniketan.

Agarwal, B. (1986), 'Women, Poverty and Agricultural Growth in India', *Journal of Peasant Studies*, vol. 14, no. 4, July.

Agarwal, B. (1994), *A field of one's own: gender and land rights in South Asia*, Cambridge University Press, Cambridge.

Akerlof and Yellen (1986), *Efficiency Wage Models of the Labour Market*, Cambridge University Press, Cambridge.

Ashenfelter, O. and Layard, R. (1986), *Handbook of Labour Economics*, vol.1. North-Holland.

Azariades (1975), 'Implicit Contracts and Underemployment Equilibria', *Journal of Political Economy*, pp. 1183-1202.

Bardhan, P. (1984), *Land, Labour and Rural Poverty*, Columbia University Press, New York.

Bardhan, P. (ed) (1989), *Conversations between Economists and Anthropologists: Methodological Issues in Measuring Economic Change in Rural India*, Oxford University Press, Delhi.

Bhattacharya, N. and Chattopadhyay, M. (1989), 'Time Trends in the Level of Living in Rural India: A Critical Study of the Evidence from Large-Scale Surveys', in Bardhan, P. (ed), *Conversations between Economists and Anthropologists: Methodological Issues in Measuring Economic Change in Rural India*, Oxford University Press, Delhi.

Biswanger, H. and Rosenzweig, M.R. (1984), *Contractual arrangements, employment and wages in rural labour markets in Asia*, Yale University Press, New Haven.

Bliss, C. J. and Stern, N. H. (1982), *Palanpur: The Economy of an Indian Village*, Oxford University Press, Delhi.

Breman, Jan (1985), *Of Peasants, Migrants and Paupers: Rural Labour Circulation and Capitalist Production in West India*, Oxford University Press, Delhi and Oxford.

Chandrasekhar, C. P. (1993), 'Agrarian Change and Occupational Diversification', *Journal of Peasant Studies*, vol. 20, no. 2, p. 205-270.

Coondoo, D. and Datta, B. (1992), 'Measurement of Income Mobility : An Application to India', in Basu, K. and Nayak, P. (ed.) *Development Policy and Economic Theory*, Oxford University Press, Delhi.

Dasgupta, P. (1993), 'An Inquiry into Well-Being and Destitution', Oxford University Press, London.

Datt, G. and Ravallion, M. (1993), 'Regional Disparities, Targetting, and Poverty in India', in Lipton, M. and Van der Gaag (eds), *Including the Poor*, Oxford University Press for the World Bank.

Dréze, J.P. and Mukherjee, A. (1987), 'Labour Contracts in Rural India : Theories and Evidence', Working Paper, Suntory-Toyota International Centre for Economics and Related Disciplines (STICERD), London School of Economics.

Dréze, J,P., Lanjouw and Stern, N.H., (1992), 'Economic Mobility and Agricultural Mobility in Rural India: A Case Study', Discussion paper No. 35, DERP, STICERD, London School of Economics.

Dréze, J. and Sen, A. (1995), *Indian Economic Development and Social Opportunity*, Clarendon Press, Oxford.

Gaiha, R. (1988a), 'On Measuring the Risk of Poverty in Rural India', in T.N. Srinivasan and P. Bardhan (eds) *Rural Poverty in South Asia*, Columbia University Press, New York.

Gaiha, R. (1988b), 'Income Mobility in Rural India', *Economic Development and Cultural Change*, pp. 279-302.

Gazdar, H. (1992), 'Rural Poverty, Public Policy and Social Change: Some Findings from Surveys of Six Villages', WIDER Working Papers, WP 98, Helsinki.

Greene, W. (1991), *Econometric Analysis*, Maxwell Macmillan International Editions, Macmillan Publishing Company, New York.

Hunt, D. (1991), 'Farm systems and household economy frameworks for prioritising and appraising technical research: a critical appraisal of current approaches', in Haswell, M. and Hunt, D., *Rural Households in Emerging Societies*, Berg, Oxford and New York.

Indra, D.M. and Buchignani, N. (1997), 'Rural Landlessness, Extended Entitlements and Inter-household Relations in South Asia: A Bangladesh Case', *Journal of Peasant Studies*, vol. 24, no. 3, pp. 25-64.

Jodha, N.S. (1989), 'Social Science Research on Rural Change: Some Gaps', in P. Bardhan (ed), *Conversations between Economists and Anthropologists: Methodological Issues in Measuring Economic Change in Rural India*, Oxford University Press, Delhi.

Jodha, N.S. (1994), 'Common Property Resources and the Environmental Contest: Role of Biological versus Social Stresses', *Economic and Political Weekly*, vol. XXX, no. 51, 23 December.

Johnson, P. (1997), 'Moving in and out of poverty', *New Economy*, vol. 4, no. 1, p. 7-11.

Lanjouw, P and Stern, N.H. (eds) (1998), *Economic Development in Palanpur Over Five Decades*, Oxford University Press, Oxford and Delhi.

Maddala, G.S. (1983), *Limited Dependent and Qualitative Variables in Econometrics*, Econometric Society Monographs, Cambridge University Press, Cambridge.

Malinvaud, E. (1977), 'The Theory of Unemployment Reconsidered', Basil Blackwell, Oxford.

Mandal, G.C. and Sengupta, S. (1962), 'Kashipur, West Bengal 1956-60: a report on resurvey of a village', *Studies of Rural Change*, AERC, Visva-Bharati, Santiniketan.

Mukherjee, A. and Ray, D. (1995), 'Labour Tying', *Journal of Development Economics*.

Mukherjee, A. and Vashishtha, P.S. (1996), 'The effects of Agricultural Price Liberalization on Rural Poverty in India', mimeo NCAER.

Pal, S. (1996), 'Workers' Self-selection in Rural Labour Markets in India', *Journal of Development Studies*, vol. 33. no. 1, pp. 99-116.

Pal, S. (1998), 'Farm Size and Hoarding Costs : Modelling Choice of Labour Contracts for Indian Agriculture', *Applied Economics,* November 1998.

Pal, S. and Kynch, J. (1998), 'Dynamics of Poverty: Occupational Mobility in Rural India', Cardiff Business School Discussion paper 98-034.

Rahman, A. (1986), *Peasants and Classes: a study in differentiation in Bangladesh*, London, Zed Press.

Reddy, C.R. (1985), 'Rural Labour Market in Varhad : A Case Study of Agricultural Labourers in Rain-Fed Agriculture in India', Working Paper, no. WEP 10-6/WP75, International Labour Office, Geneva.

Rogaly, B. (1996), 'Agricultural Growth and the Structure of 'Casual' Labour-Hiring in Rural West Bengal', *Journal of Peasant Studies*, vol. 23, no. 4, pp. 141-165.

Rogaly, B. (1997),'Dangerous Liaisons? Seasonal Labour Migration and Agrarian Change in West Bengal' in Rogaly, B., B. Harriss-White and S. Bose (ed.) *Sonar Bangla? Agricultural Growth and Agrarian Change in West Bengal and Bangladesh* (forthcoming).

Schmidt, P. and R. P. Strauss (1975), 'The Prediction of Occupation Using Multiple Logit Models', *International Economic Review*, p. 471-486.

Scott, C.D. and J. A. Litchfield (1994), 'Inequality, Mobility and the Determinants of Income Among the Rural Poor in Chile, 1968-86', Discussion Paper no. 53, Development Economics Research Programme, STICERD, London School of Economics.

Sen, Amartya (1975), *Employment, Technology and Development*, Clarendon Press, Oxford.

Sen, Amartya and Sunil Sengupta 1983. 'Malnutrition of Rural Children and the Sex Bias', *Economic and Political Weekly*, 19 (Annual Number).

Sengupta, Sunil and H Gazdar (1997), 'Agrarian Politics and Rural Development in West Bengal', in Dreze and Sen (eds), *Indian Development: Selected Regional Perspectives*, Oxford University Press, Oxford and New Delhi.

Shanin, T. (1972), *The Awkward Class*, Penguin.

Vaidyanathan, A. (1989), 'Macro and Micro Approaches to Studying Rural Economic Change: Some Pointers from Indian Experience', in Bardhan, P. (ed), *Conversations between Economists and Anthropologists: Methodological Issues in Measuring Economic Change in Rural India*, Oxford University Press, Delhi.

Van Schendel, W. (1981), *Peasant Mobility: The odds of life in rural Bangladesh*, Assen, van Gorcum.

Walker, R. (1995), 'The dynamics of poverty and social exclusion', in Room, G. (ed), *Beyond the Threshold: the Measurement and Analysis of Social Exclusion*, Bristol: The Policy Press, WIDER 1989.

Walker, T.S. and Ryan, J.G. (1990), *Village and Household Economies in India's Semi-arid Tropics*, John Hopkins University Press, Baltimore and London.

PART V
ECONOMIC IDEAS

8 P N Mathur and the Theory of Layers of Technique

T AZID AND D GHOSH

Professor P.N. Mathur's death in 1993 deprived economics of one of its most distinguished members. During his career he published over a hundred papers, many of them substantial, pioneering contributions to various areas of economics. All his work was original. What he developed theoretically he proved empirically.

His principal contributions are to be found in the areas of Development Economics, Agricultural Economics, Input-Output Analysis, and the theory of the layers of technique. In much of his work he used the Indian Economy as his test bed. This chapter concentrates on his contribution to the theory of layers of technique. This work draws very much on related work in other areas.

The Theory of Layers of Technique

Professor Mathur's approach to layers of technique, which he defined as a spectrum of techniques or techniques of different vintages with different productive efficiencies, working simultaneously in an industry. In his economy, the opportunity cost of fixed capital, once installed, is equal to zero. Fixed capital is not, in his view, a meccano set that can be pulled apart and reconstructed. In his view there is no point in calculating or developing a methodology for calculating of the value of fixed capital after its installation. These considerations should be given only to working capital, because it is easily transferable from one production process to another. In this construct, the least efficient technique (the technique of the oldest vintage) determines the price of the product, accruing a zero pseudo quasi-rent. The price of a product is then equal to the variable cost per unit of output produced by the least efficient technique plus a mark-up. While the most recent technique (best practised or the latest vintage) earns the highest pseudo quasi-rent. Note that prices of manufacturing goods, in this framework, are determined in *the*

Hicksian fix price framework. A technique can only survive in this world when the price of the product does not fall below its average variable cost, otherwise it will be abandoned or scrapped. Firms still using the technique will either voluntarily exit the industry or be forced out by bankruptcy.

In the real world, a technique of a particular vintage exists simultaneously with a number of other techniques each having its own distinct productive efficiency. Every "latest" technique is more efficient than the preceding one. Those techniques that have the highest, average and zero pseudo quasi-rent are conceived respectively as 'Best', 'Average' and 'Marginal' techniques. Marginal techniques are on the verge of obsolescence. Pseudo quasi-rent is the difference between the prevailing price of the product (average revenue) and its average variable cost. In this fluid economic milieu, the best practice technique of today is the average technique of tomorrow and the average of today is the marginal of tomorrow. As a result the reality of layers of techniques determines the industrial structure of an economy.

Pseudo Quasi-Rent

Mathur's concept of pseudo quasi-rent needs some explanation. It can be compared to Schumpeter's profit, Ricardo's rent and Marshallian quasi-rent but there are differences. To some extent it is like Schumpeter's profit, though a bit more comprehensive. Schumpeter's profit exclude interest payments and depreciation on fixed capital, while depreciation and the interest on the fixed capital are included in pseudo quasi-rent. It may be worth emphasising that quasi-rent and Schumpeterian profit are technological phenomena and are defined for a given price structure and thus should be distinguished from the commonly understood concept of profit which is the result of changes and fluctuations in the price structure itself.

Pseudo quasi-rent is almost like Ricardo's rent. Like rent, it is based on differentiated efficiency of different units and is equivalent to the difference between the earnings of various units from that of the 'marginal' unit. Both are surpluses which do not affect firms production decisions in the short run. If we think in terms of long-run, however, the two concepts diverge. Over time, as new techniques arise with each more efficient than previous one firms adopting these earn more pseudo quasi-rent. In Ricardo's theory of land-rent the units of highest productivity come in to production first and with time, as more and more units, each successively of poorer quality than the one before, come into production the rental income of the better quality units keep on rising. It is the unit which was pressed into production last that covers the cost of production and earns no rent. In Mathur's system it is the unit introduced last into production that earns the rent.

The relationship between the Marshallian quasi-rent and pseudo quasi-rent is as follows. Marshallian quasi-rent is the result of a lag between the rise in the demand for an existing product and the establishment of new firms to satisfy this additional demand. At a given point in time, therefore, all existing firms can earn the same quasi-rent and a new firm is not in any particularly advantageous position over its predecessors in this respect. In Mathur's system a new firm or an old firm using the latest technique is likely to earn more pseudo quasi-rent than its predecessors because it can take advantage of new technologies.

Vintage Capital and Price Behaviour

Professor Mathur developed an input-output model for estimating the input-output coefficients of an economy using techniques of different vintages. From this he calculated the effect of this on price formulation. His model estimated the obsolescence of different existing techniques.

Professor Mathur and Professor A. P. Carter were the pioneers who introduced the element of structural change into the dynamic input-output framework under the assumption that new techniques are embodied in capital. At that time very little was known about new- technology input structures. There was no clear picture of rapidly changing input-output structures in general. It was not then possible for either of them to appraise the relevance or the merits of this approach in analysing the operation of the economy as a whole. Professor Mathur's primary emphasis was theoretical and he had to restrict his empirical application to a hypothetical example. Here the United States input-output structure for 1947 was used to represent the 'best-practice' structure which needed to be adopted to generate new capacity for the Indian economy in all sectors. Later on, as new and better information become available, Professor Mathur continued to work on this theme and ultimately constructed "marginal" input-output coefficients from cross-section data without taking fixed capital into account. These marginal coefficients represented both spectrums of the economic sectors, i.e., the worst and the best practise techniques. He observed that there was a large gap between the average and marginal input-output tables. In his view when we want to estimate the implications of an increase or a decrease in final demand or the implications of fiscal or monetary changes on the price structure we require the use of "marginal" input-output tables. This is because "marginal" input-output coefficients not only depict the most efficient techniques but the least efficient ones as well. He also estimated the worse and the best coefficient for each existing technique for every sector. Indeed these "marginal" input-output coefficients allow input-output analysis to meet the challenge of precision especially in the area of forecasting.

Concept of Efficiency

Mathur developed independently a method for the measurement of factor productivity and the efficiency of firms based on average variable cost. According to him the traditional method for the measurement of (single or multi) factor productivity and neo-classical production function was totally irrelevant for practical purposes including that of policy formulation. His method attempted to measure the productivity of the factors of production associated with different techniques. The advantage of this method is that for forecasting purposes it is useful to ascertain which technique is on the verge of obsolescence, in order to arrive at the future price structure and the failure rate of firms. The concepts of efficiency as measured by labour productivity, total factor productivity, and the production function are fundamentally different from that measured by average variable cost. Even between themselves these three measures of efficiency measure different things. While the total factor productivity and production function try to approximate overall efficiency, the average variable cost measure tries to gauge the survival potential of firms. These two concepts are very different. While the former is important when we are putting up a new establishment, the latter becomes useful when the fixed capital is already sunk and is beyond retrieval. This measure also reveals how an existing establishment is facing its current competitors in the accounting sense. This matters for the firm when deciding whether to continue operating or close down. When an establishment finds itself on the verge of unfeasibility, its decision to close down will not depend on whether it is getting any returns on fixed capital which is irretrievably gone, but on whether it is able to meet its working expenses. That is, not when its overall productivity has become negative but when its survival efficiency or potential becomes negative.

Effect of Interest Rates on the Economy with Several Layers of Techniques

Mathur developed a theory regarding the rate of interest compatible with the coexistence of several layers of techniques. He explained that interest rates provide mechanism for determining the obsolescence of a technology. In an economy where fixed capital exists corresponding to the technologies of various vintages, obsolescence is determined by the necessity of meeting the limited demand for goods by the most efficient of the technologies embodied in capital goods. Thus determination of interest rates in an intense state of flux turns out to be a short term phenomenon dependent on the real part of the economy. This gives a real independent basis for determining the short term rate of interest which need not be an approximation of the long run one, as envisaged by Fisher (1930), for whom only the long term interest rate was the natural phenomenon.

When an economy has capital goods of several vintages simultaneously working to produce the output it requires, it takes the help of the interest rate mechanism to signal the dated capital goods whose output is not required by the economy. The higher are interest rates the greater the reduction in the amount of capacity. On the other hand an increase in the price of goods over the production period increases the pseudo quasi-rent making it possible to increase capacity which may produce more goods and/or allows a higher nominal rate to be earned. Looked at it in another way, an increase in the interest rates charged by the banks may reduce the economy's total output and employment by making marginal techniques economically obsolete and/or create inflationary pressures to compensate for higher interest payments producers may increase prices. In practice, in the face of a rise in short term interest rate, both types of adjustments will operate. Some marginal techniques will cease to operate creating some degree of unemployment although the whole adjustment may not be done in that way. Some part of the adjustment will be done by the inflationary mechanism. It will all depend on how much demand can be squeezed out of the system. If demand can be squeezed sufficiently, the higher interest rate would just reduce the capacity that can work profitably. If not it will be the rise in prices that will meet the requirements of the rise in the nominal interest rates. So in general we may expect the effect of increases in interest rates to be partly reflected in the rise in prices and partly in a decreases in output and consequently in unemployment.

Non-Abandonment by Firms

A very interesting concept which Mathur developed from US data, regarding the non abandonment by firms whose average variable cost is higher than the prevailing price. In this world of uncertainty, it is difficult for an entrepreneur to decide in the very short run whether to enter or exit an industry. In reality, it is not a decision which can be taken quickly. It takes time and is influenced by several crucial factors. In the Marshallian world, if a firm is experiencing operating losses it will decide to exit the industry and when observing the existence of supernormal profits in the industry it will decide to enter. On the contrary, in the real world the phenomenon of abandonment is not observed as in the Marshallian world. It has been seen that firms stay in business for a while, when experiencing operating losses.

According to Mathur, firms do not leave an industry in the short run for a combination of the following:

(1) *Transfer of Technology*: Producers will attempt to transfer fixed capital to a region, (which might be within the country) where variable costs are lower. This could be due to such reasons as favourable infrastructure, low wage cost and so on. Producers may transfer fixed capital to an underdeveloped country to take advantage of cheap labour and other such factors. These may include subsidised inputs such as electricity.

(2) *Working Capital:* Sometimes it is very difficult to withdraw the working capital from the production process when the process is continuing, so the producers wait until they can withdraw the working capital. This is not, however, due to any expectations about the future and is not a long term consideration for producers.

(3) *Retrofitting*: It is observed in industry, that some improvements in the production process on a small scale basis (retrofitting) increase the efficiency of firms and enables them to obtain a positive pseudo quasi-rent. This provides another impetus for firms to continue working, even in the face of operating losses. In the intermediate period, when firms are retrofitting, the producers cannot close their firms because they cannot take the risk of loosing their trained labour force which is usually very specific to the industry concerned or their markets.

According to the layers of technique approach, firms do not stay in business because they expect that economic conditions will improve in the future. It is irrational for them to continue to suffer operating losses in the hope that the future will be better. It is more likely that firms will respond in a strategic way. Waiting is not a solution even when future expectations look positive. To the contrary rational producers are those, who are constantly trying to meet the challenges presented to them by economic events and so limit losses as much as they can. If producers can withdraw the working capital without any obstruction then they might embark upon a search for finding a new home for their investment and/or use for their obsolete *(economically* but not *physically)* fixed capital. Where variable cost per unit of output is low retrofitting is a possible solution. If they find that none of the above alternatives are feasible then it is obviously better for them to shut down and leave the industry. This strategic approach can help to explain the behaviour of multi-national corporations who transfer their dated technologies (plants) to countries in the Third World as part of collaborative joint ventures with local companies.

In the changing economic environment at any given moment in time, a spectrum of techniques exists working simultaneously with different productive efficiencies. Best practice techniques (those of the latest vintages) are entering the market while marginal techniques (of old vintages) which are on the verge of obsolescence are leaving the market. The existence of old techniques depends on the state of demand in the economy. If demand does not increase in line with the creation of new capacity then over capacity will arise. Producers employing marginal techniques will then be faced with the decision whether to carry on or exit the industry. Waiting for something to turn up Mcorber like is not an option. producers will have to act strategically in the longer term even if the continue to operate at a loss in the short run.

Conclusions

Mathur's development of the idea of layers of technique gives us some important insights into the workings of the economic system. His concept of pseudo-quasi rent explains the simultaneous existence of different vintages of technology in an industry at any particular period of time. It also suggests that the structure of prices in an industry will be set by the marginal technique. As long as price covers the average variable costs of production of the marginal technique then those firms employing newer techniques are earning pseudo-quasi rents if they sell their goods at that price. In order to capture more pseudo-quasi rents producers will be encouraged to invest in newer and, therefore, more productive and profitable techniques. Those producers using older vintages will react to these competitive pressures by either transferring their old capital to areas which offer lower operating costs, or carry out some retrofitting, or if the pressures are too great withdraw their working capital when the opportunity arises.

Mathur's ideas also provide us with an insight into company pricing behaviour when faced with changing macroeconomic conditions. When interest rates increase a company will attempt to pass on these increased costs in the form of higher prices. This will be done in order to maintain its returns to capital. If producers cannot carry this out then those using marginal techniques for production will be forced out of business.

References

Fisher, I. (1930), *The Theory of Interest*, Macmillan, London.

PART VI
CONCLUSIONS

9 Conclusions

It is now just over fifty years since India gained its independence from Britain. During this period India has seen many changes both in the economic and social spheres. In many ways, however, one can say that India's fundamental problems have remained the same. It is still concerned principally with the alleviation of poverty via the promotion of economic growth. If the principal concerns of the Indian State have not changed what has is the context in which they are being addressed. In the early years of independence and until very recently the main thrust of development was the promotion of domestic industries via a closed economy model supported by state planning. This resulted in a panoply of exchange rate restrictions, multiple exchange rates, high tariff barriers and bilateral trade negotiations. Public sector involvement was high in the modern industrial sectors.

The current attitude to the promotion of development emphasises exchange rate and trade liberalisation and the promotion of private enterprise especially amongst areas formally restricted to government involvement. This contextual change is reflected clearly in this volume's chapters. Ghatak and Siddiki addressed the issue of exchange rates, Kerr, Perdikis and Hobbs the potential liberalisation for expanding trade between India and the NAFTA countries. Murshed and Perdikis examined the changing pattern of trade between India and the EU. Nixon and Arun discussed the movement towards privatisation and its impact on telecommunications and power generation. Kynch and Pal also examined the traditional issue of poverty in a new light. While environmental considerations can be considered as new in some respects have always figured in discussions in India. Here the paper by Chakravarty and Reddy suggested that the solution to India's environmental problems are better sought in an international and co-operative context.

The final chapter in the book deals with the development of the ideas of P N Mathur, in particular his contribution to the theory of "layers of technique". Here we are exposed to his view of rent which contrasts with that of Ricardo. Mathur's analysis provides us with additional insights into a company's behaviour towards production, investment, pricing and location. Mathur's ideas are not only contemporary contributions to economics they can be seen as part of a long Indian tradition.

Bibliography

Adams, R., Adams, D., Callaway, J., Chang, C. and McCarl, B. (1993), 'Sequestering Carbon on Agricultural Land: Social Cost and Impacts on Timber Markets', *Contemporary Political Issues*, vol. 11, no.1, pp. 76-87.

AERC (1988), 'Employment conditions and modes of wage payments of agricultural labour in Birbhum, West Bengal', Agro-Economic Research Centre, Visva-Bharati, Santiniketan.

AERC (various), *Studies in Rural Change*, Reports on surveys and re-surveys of villages in West Bengal, Agro-Economic Research Centre, Visva-Bharati, Santiniketan.

Agarwal, B. (1986), 'Women, Poverty and Agricultural Growth in India', *Journal of Peasant Studies*, vol. 14, no. 4, July.

Agarwal, B. (1994), *A field of one's own: gender and land rights in South Asia*, Cambridge University Press, Cambridge.

Agenor, Pierre-Richard (1990), 'Stabilisation Policies in Developing Countries with a Parallel Market for Foreign Exchange: A Formal Framework', *IMF Staff Papers*, vol.37, no. 3, pp. 560-592.

Agenor, Pierre-Richard (1991), 'A Monetary Model of the Parallel Market for Foreign Exchange', *Journal of Economic Studies*, vol. 18, no. 4, pp. 4-18.

Akerlof and Yellen (1986), *Efficiency Wage Models of the Labour Market*, Cambridge University Press, Cambridge.

Ambrose,W. Hennemeyer, P.R. and Chapon, J.P. (1990), 'Privatising Telecommunication Systems: Business Opportunities in Developing Countries', IFC Discussion Paper no.10, The World Bank and IFC, Washington DC.

Anderson, W. (1996), 'India in 1995', *Asian Survey*, vol. 36, no. 2, pp. 165-178.

Aquino, A. (1978), 'Intra-industry trade and intra-industry specialisation as concurrent sources of international trade in manufactures', *Weltwirtschaftliches Archiv*. vol.114.

Arun, T.G. and Nixson, F.I. (1997), 'Privatisation and Foreign participation - The Indian experience', *Journal of the Asia Pacific Economy*, vol. 2, no. 2, 1997, pp. 201-224.

Arun, T.G. and Nixson, F.I. (1998a), 'The Transition of a Public sector monopoly: India's experience with Telecommunications', *Journal of International Development*, vol. 10, no. 3, John Wiley & Sons, Ltd.

Arun, T.G. and Nixson, F.I. (1998b), 'The Reform of the Power sector in India: 1991-1997', *Journal of International Development*, vol. 10, no. 4, John Wiley & Sons, Ltd.

Arun, T.G. and Nixson, F.I. (1999), 'Disinvestment of Public sector enterprises: The Indian Experience', *Oxford Development Studies* (forthcoming).

Ashenfelter, O. and Layard, R. (1986), *Handbook of Labour Economics*, vol.1. North-Holland.

Azariades (1975), 'Implicit Contracts and Underemployment Equilibria', *Journal of Political Economy*, pp. 1183-1202.

Bardhan, P. (1984), *Land, Labour and Rural Poverty*, Columbia University Press, New York.

Bardhan, P. (ed) (1989), *Conversations between Economists and Anthropologists: Methodological Issues in Measuring Economic Change in Rural India*, Oxford University Press, Delhi.

Barret, S. (1994), 'Self-Enforcing International Environmental Agreements', *Oxford Economic Papers*, vol. 46, pp. 878-894.

Bhattacharya, N. and Chattopadhyay, M. (1989), 'Time Trends in the Level of Living in Rural India: A Critical Study of the Evidence from Large-Scale Surveys', in P. Bardhan (ed), *Conversations between Economists and Anthropologists: Methodological Issues in Measuring Economic Change in Rural India*, Oxford University Press, Delhi.

Bienen, H. and Waterbury J. (1989), 'The Political Economy of Privatisation in Developing Countries' in *World Development*, vol. 17, no. 5, pp. 617-632.

Biswanger, H. and Rosenzweig, M.R. (1984), *Contractual arrangements, employment and wages in rural labour markets in Asia*, Yale University Press, New Haven.

Blejer, M.L. (1978), 'Exchange Restrictions and the Monetary Approach to the Exchange Rate', in Frankel, J.A. and Johnson, H.G. (eds), *The Economics of Exchange Rates: Selected Studies*, Reading, MA.

Bliss, C. J. and Stern, N. H. (1982), *Palanpur: The Economy of an Indian Village*, Oxford University Press, Delhi.

Bos, D. (1991), *Privatisation: A Theoretical Treatment*, Clarendon Press, Oxford.

Breman, Jan (1985), *Of Peasants, Migrants and Paupers: Rural Labour Circulation and Capitalist Production in West India*, Oxford University Press, Delhi and Oxford.

Brown, R., Durbin, J. and Evans, J. (1975), 'Techniques for Testing the Constancy of Regression Relationships over Time', *Journal of Royal Statistical Society, Series B*, vol. 37, pp. 149-172.

Brülhart, M. (1994), 'Marginal Intra-industry Trade: Measurement and Relevance for the pattern of adjustment', *Weltwirtschaftliches Archiv.* vol.130.

Brülhart, M. and McAleese, D. (1995) 'Intra-industry trade and Industrial Adjustment in Ireland,' *The Economic and Social Review*, vol.26, no.2.

Chaemza, W.W. and Ghatak, S. (1990), 'Demand for Money in Dual-Currency Quantity-Constrined Economy: Hungary and Poland, 1956-85', *The Economic Journal*, vol. 100, pp. 1159-1172.

Chandrasekhar, C. P. (1993), 'Agrarian Change and Occupational Diversification', *Journal of Peasant Studies*, vol. 20, no. 2, p. 205-70.

Charemza, W.W. (1990), 'Parallel Markets, Excess Demand and Virtual Prices: An Empirical Approach', *European Economic Review*, vol. 34, pp. 331-339.

Cline W.R. (1992), *The Economics of Global Warming*, Washington, D.C.: Institute for International Economics.

Cook, P. and Kirkpatrick, C. (1988), 'Privatisation in Less Developed Countries: An Overview' in Cook, P. and Kirkpatrick, C. (eds.), *Privatisation in Less Developed Countries,* Harvester Wheatsheaf, New York.

Coondoo, D. and Datta, B. (1992), 'Measurement of Income Mobility : An Application to India', in Basu, K. and Nayak, P. (ed.) *Development Policy and Economic Theory*, Oxford University Press, Delhi.

Cowan, G.L. (1990), *Privatisation in the Developing World*, Praeger, New York.

Cowitt, Phillips P. (various years), *World Currency Yearbook*, International Currency Analysis, Brooklyn, New York.

Culbertson, W.P. Jr., (1975), 'Purchasing Power Parity and the Black Market Exchange Rates', *Economic Inquiry*, vol. XIII, pp. 250-257.

Culbertson, W.P. Jr., (1989) 'Empirical Regularities in Black Markets for Currency', *World Development*, vol. 17, pp. 1907-1919.

Dasgupta, P. (1993), 'An Inquiry into Well-Being and Destitution', Oxford University Press, London.

Datt, G. and Ravallion, M. (1993), 'Regional Disparities, Targetting, and Poverty in India', in Lipton, M. and Van der Gaag (eds), *Including the Poor*, Oxford University Press for the World Bank.

Datt, R. (1995), 'New Economic Reforms - Need for Some Re-thinking', *The Indian Economic Journal*, vol. 42, no. 3, pp. 92-113.

Dixon R., Winjum J. and Krakina, O. (1991), 'Afforestation and Forest Management Optionsand Their Costs at the Site Level', in IIED (eds), *Proceedings of the Technical Workshop to Explore Options for Global Forestry Management*, April 24-30, Bangkok, Thailand.

Dornbusch, R. (1993), *Policy Making in the Open Economy*, Oxford University Press, England.

Dornbusch, R., Dantas, D.V., Pechman, C., Rocha, R.R. and Simoes, D. (1983), 'The Black Market for Dollars in Brazil', *Quarterly Journal of Economics*, vol. 98, pp. 25-40.

Drèze, J,P., Lanjouw and Stern, N.H. (1992), 'Economic Mobility and Agricultural Mobility in Rural India: A Case Study', Discussion paper No. 35, DERP, STICERD, London School of Economics.

Drèze, J. and Sen, A. (1995), *Indian Economic Development and Social Opportunity*, Clarendon Press, Oxford.

Drèze, J.P., and Mukherjee, A. (1987), 'Labour Contracts in Rural India : Theories and Evidence', Working Paper, Suntory-Toyota International Centre for Economics and Related Disciplines (STICERD), London School of Economics.

Dutt, A.K. (1997), 'Uncertain Success: The Political Economy of Indian Economic Reform', *Journal of International Affairs*, vol. 51, no.1

EIU (1998), *Foreign investment in India: Opportunities and obstacles*, The Economist Intelligence Unit, London.

Engle, R.F. and Granger, C.W.J. (1987), 'Cointegration and Error Correction: Representation, Estimation and Testing', *Econometrica*, 52, 251-76.

Escapa, M. and Gutierrez, M.J. (1997), 'Distribution of Potential Gains from International Environmental Agreements: The Case of the Greenhouse Effect', *Journal of Environmental Economics and Management*, vol. 33, pp. 1-16.

Fairman, D. and Ross, M. (1996), 'Old Fads, New Lessons: Learning from Economic Development Assistance', pp. 29-52, in Keohane, Robert O. and Levy, Marc A. (eds), *Institutions for Environmental Aid*, MIT Press, Cambridge, Mass.

Fankhauser, S. (1994), 'The Social Cost of Greenhouse Emissions: An Expected Value Approach', *Energy Journal*, vol. 15, No. 2, pp. 157-184.

Fankhauser, S. (1995), *Valuing Climate Change: Economics of Greenhouse* Earthscan, London.

Fisher, I. (1930), *The Theory of Interest*, Macmillan, London.

Furubotn, E.G. and Pejovich, S. (1972), 'Property rights and economic theory: a survey of recent literature', *Journal of Economic Literature*, vol. 10, no.4.

Gaiha, R. (1988a), 'On Measuring the Risk of Poverty in Rural India', in Srinivasan, T.N. and Bardhan, P. (eds) *Rural Poverty in South Asia*, Columbia University Press, New York.

Gaiha, R. (1988b), 'Income Mobility in Rural India', *Economic Development and Cultural Change*, pp. 279-302.

Gazdar, H. (1992), 'Rural Poverty, Public Policy and Social Change: Some Findings from Surveys of Six Villages', WIDER Working Papers, WP 98, Helsinki.

Ghatak, A. and Ghatak, S. (1996), 'Budgetary Deficits and Recardian Equivalence: The Case of India', *Journal of Public Economics*, vol. 60, pp. 267-282.

Ghosh, B. and Neogi, C. (1996), 'Liberalization in India: Quality Differentiates Between Public and Private Employees', *The Developing Economies*, vol. 34, no. 1, pp. 61-79.

Globerman, S., Kokko, A., Revelius, M. and Sami, M. (1996), 'MNE Responses to Economic Liberalization in a Developing Country: Evidence from India', *Journal of Economic Development*, vol. 21, no. 2, pp. 163-184.

GOI (1989), *Report of the Working Group for Wasteland Development Sector in the Eighth Five Year Plan*, Ministry of Environment and Forests, New Delhi.

GOI (1994a), *National Telecom Policy*, Government of India, 13-05-1994.

GOI (1994b), *Private Investment in Power sector: Myths and Realities*, Ministry of Power, Government of India.

GOI (1996), *Handbook of Industrial Policy and Statistics*, Ministry of Industry, Government of India.

GOI (1996-98), Disinvestment Commission Reports I-VIII, Ministry of Industry, Government of India.

GOI (1997), *Economic Survey 1996-97*, Ministry of Finance, Government of India.

GOI (1999), *Economic Survey 1998-99*, Ministry of Finance, Government of India.

Gouri, G. (1996), 'Privatisation and public sector enterprises in India: analysis of impact of a non-policy', *Economic and Political Weekly*, 30 November, M63-M74.

Granger, C.W.J. (1988), 'Some Recent Development in the Concept of Causality', *Journal of Econometrics*, vol. 39, pp. 199-211.

Greenaway, D. and Milner, C. (1986), *The Economics of Intra-industry trade*, Basil Blackwell, Oxford.

Greene, W. (1991), *Econometric Analysis*, Maxwell Macmillan International Editions, Macmillan Publishing Company, New York.

Grubel, H.J. and Lloyd, P.J. (1975) *Intra-industry trade: The Theory and Measurement of International Trade in Differentiated Products*, John Wiley & Sons, New York.

Gupta, S. (1980), 'An Application of the Monetary Approach to Black Market Exchange Rates', *Welwirtschaftliches Archiv*, vol. 116, pp 235-52.

Harris-White, B. (1996), 'Liberalization and Corruption', *IDS Bulletin*, vol. 27, no. 2, pp. 31-39.

Haurylyshyn, O. and Civan, E. (1983), 'Intra-industry trade and the stage of development', in Tharakan, P.K.M. (1983), *Intra-industry trade, Empirical and Methodological Aspects*, Chapter 5, North Holland, Amsterdam.

Helpman, E. and Krugman, P. (1985), *Market Structure and Foreign Trade*, Harvester Wheatsheaf, Brighton.

Hendry, D.F. (1989), *PC GIVE: An Interactive Modelling System*, Oxford University Press, England.

Hendry, D.F. and Richards, J.F. (1982), 'On the Formulation of Empirical Models of Dynamic Econometrics', *Journal of Econometrics*, vol. 29, no. 3, pp. 3-33.

Hunt, D. (1991), 'Farm systems and household economy frameworks for prioritising and appraising technical research: a critical appraisal of current approaches', in Haswell, M. and Hunt, D., *Rural Households in Emerging Societies*, Berg, Oxford and New York.

Indra, D.M. and Buchignani, N. (1997), 'Rural Landlessness, Extended Entitlements and Inter-household Relations in South Asia: A Bangladesh Case', *Journal of Peasant Studies*, vol. 24, no. 3, pp. 25-64.

International Monetary Fund (1997), *Exchange Arrangements and Exchange Restrictions: Annual Report 1997*, Washington, D.C.

IPPC (1996), *Climate Change 1995 - Impacts, Adaptations and Mitigation of Climate Change: Scientific-Technical Analysis, Contributions of Working Group II to the Second Assessment Report of the Intergovernmental Panel on Climate Change*, Cambridge University Press, Cambridge.

Iqbal, B.A. (1994), 'Will India's External Sector Sustain the Economy?', *India Quarterly*, vol. 50 nos. 1-2, pp. 123-134.

Iqbal, B.A. and Khan, A.O. (1994), 'TCNs: India in a World Perspective', *India Quarterly*, vol. 50, no. 3, pp. 95-102.

Jodha, N.S. (1989), 'Social Science Research on Rural Change: Some Gaps', in Bardhan, P. (ed), *Conversations between Economists and Anthropologists: Methodological Issues in Measuring Economic Change in Rural India*, Oxford University Press, Delhi.

Jodha, N.S. (1994), 'Common Property Resources and the Environmental Contest: Role of Biological versus Social Stresses', *Economic and Political Weekly*, vol. XXX, no. 51, 23 December.

Johnson, P. (1997), 'Moving in and out of poverty', *New Economy*, vol. 4, no. 1, p. 7-11.

Jones, J.D. and Joulifain, D. (1991), 'Federal Government Expenditures and Revenues in the Early Years of the American Republic: Evidence from 1792 to 1860', *Journal of Macroeconomics*, vol. 13, pp. 133-55.

Kaplinsky, R. (1997), 'India's Industrial Development: An Interpretative Survey', *World Development*, vol. 25, no. 5, pp. 681-694.

Kautilya (278 BC), *Arthasastra*, Translated by Dr. R. Shamasastry, Wesleyan Mission Press, 1923.

Kerr, W.A. and Anderson, C.L. (1992), 'Multinational Corporations, Local Enterprises and the Political Economy of Development - Some Basic Dynamics', *Journal of Economic Development*, vol. 10, no. 1, pp. 105-124.

Kerr, W.A. and Perdikis, N. (1995), *The Economics of International Business*, Chapman and Hall, London.

Khan, M.S. and Jonathan, D.O. (1992), 'Response of Equilibrium Real Exchange Rate to Real Disturbance in Developing Countries', *World Development*, vol. 20, pp. 1325-34.

Kochanek, S.A. (1996), 'Liberalization and Business Lobbying in India', *Journal of Commonwealth and Contemporary Politics*, vol. 34, no. 3, pp. 155-173.

Krueger, A. (1974), 'The Political Economy of Rent-Seeking Society', *American Economic Review*, vol. 44, pp. 291-303.

Lanjouw, P and Stern, N.H. (eds) (1998), *Economic Development in Palanpur Over Five Decades*, Oxford University Press, Oxford and Delhi.

Mabey, N., Hall, S., Smith, C. and Gupta, S. (1997), *Argument in the Greenhouse: The International Economics of Controlling Global Warming*, Routledge, London.

Maddala, G.S. (1983), *Limited Dependent and Qualitative Variables in Econometrics*, Econometric Society Monographs, Cambridge University Press, Cambridge.

Majumdar, K.S. and Ahuja, G. (1997), 'Privatisation: An Exegesis of Key Ideas' in *Economic and Political Weekly*, July 5: 1590-95.

Malinvaud, E. (1977), '*The Theory of Unemployment Reconsidered*', Basil Blackwell, Oxford.

Mandal, G.C. and Sengupta, S. (1962), 'Kashipur, West Bengal 1956-60: a report on resurvey of a village', *Studies of Rural Change*, AERC, Visva-Bharati, Santiniketan.

Marathe, S. (1986), *Regulation and Development India's Policy Experience of Controls over Industry*, Sage, New Delhi.

Masera, O., Bellon, M. and Segura, G. (1994), 'Forest Management Options for Sequestering Carbon in Mexico', *Biomass and Bioenergy*, vol. 8, no. 5, pp. 345-352.

Mecedo, J.S., de (1982), 'Exchange Rate Behaviour with Currency Inconvertibility', *Journal of International Economics*, vol. 12, pp. 65-81.

Mecedo, J.S., de (1987), 'Currency Inconvertibility, Trade Taxes and Smuggling', *Journal of Development Economics*, vol. 27, pp. 109-25.

Mishra R.K., Nandagopal, R. and Lateef Syed Mohammed, A. (1993), 'Sale of public enterprise shares: frittering away the nation's wealth', *Economic and Political Weekly*, 27 Novenmebr, M 163-8.

Mishra, T.K. (1992), 'India's Foreign Trade: Lessons and Challenges', *India Quarterly*, vol. 48, nos. 1-2, pp. 49-58.

Mishra, T.K. (1994), 'Task of Attracting Foreign Investment in India', *India Quarterly*, vol. 50, no. 3, pp. 107-114.

Montiel, Peter J. and Ostry, Jonathan D. (1994), 'The Parallel Market Premium: Is it a Reliable Indictor of Real Exchange Rate Misalignment in Developing Countries?', *IMF Staff Papers*, vol. 41, no. 1, pp. 55-76.

Mukherjee, A and Ray, D. (1995), 'Labour Tying', *Journal of Development Economics*.

Mukherjee, A and Vashishtha, P.S. (1996), 'The effects of Agricultural Price Liberalization on Rural Poverty in India', mimeo NCAER.

Murshed, S.M. and Noonan D. (1996) 'The quality and pattern of Intra-Industry Trade between the Geographically Proximate Regions of Northern-Southern Ireland and Southern Ireland and Great Britain,' *The Economic and Social Review*, vol.27, no.3.

Neary, P. and Roberts, K.W.S. (1980), 'The Theory of Household Behaviour Under Rationing', *European Economic Review*, vol. 13, pp. 25-42.

Nordhaus, W. D. (1991), 'To Slow or Not to Slow: The Economics of the Greenhouse Effect', *The Economics Journal*, vol.101, pp. 920-937.

OECD (1997), *The OECD report on Regulatory Reform*, vol.1 and 2, Paris.

Ogus, A. (1996), *Regulation: Legal Form and Economic Theory*, Clarendon Law series, Oxford University Press.

Pal, S. (1996), 'Workers' Self-selection in Rural Labour Markets in India', *Journal of Development Studies*, vol. 33. no. 1, pp. 99-116.

Pal, S. (1998), 'Farm Size and Hoarding Costs : Modelling Choice of Labour Contracts for Indian Agriculture', *Applied Economics*, November 1998.

Pal, S. and Kynch, J. (1998), 'Dynamics of Poverty: Occupational Mobility in Rural India', Cardiff Business School Discussion paper 98-034.

Parikh, K. (1995), 'Enron episode: Lessons for power policy', *Economic and Political Weekly*, October 14-21, 1995.

Patil, S.H. (1993), 'Collapse of Communism and Emergence of Global Economy: India's Experiment with New Economic Policy', *India Quarterly*, vol. 49, no. 4, pp. 17-30.

Patnaik, J.K. (1992), 'India and the TRIPs: Some Notes on the Uruguay Round Negotiations', *India Quarterly*, vol. 48, no. 4, pp. 31-42.

Peck, S.C. and Tiesberg, T.J. (1992), 'CETA: A Model for Carbon Emissions Trajectory Assessment', *Energy Journal*, vol. 13, no. 1, pp. 55-77.

Pesaran, H.M. and Pesaran, B. (1997), *Microfit 4.0*, Oxford University Press, England.

Pesaran, H.M. and Shin, Y. (1995), 'An Autoregressive Distributed Lag Modelling Approach to Cointegratin Analysis', DAE Working Paper Series, No. 9514, Department of Applied Economics, Cambridge University.

Pesaran, H.M., Shin, Y. and Smith, R.J. (1996), 'Testing the Existence of a Long-Run Relationship, DAE Working Paper Series, 9622, Department of Applied Economics, Cambridge University.

Phylaktis, K. (1995), 'Exchange Rate Policies in Developing Countries', in Ghatak, S., *Monetary Economics in Developing Countries*, Macmillan Press Ltd, England.

Pick, F. (Various issues) *Pick's Currency Year Book*, Pick Publishing corporation, New York.

Price, C. (1990), 'The Allowable Burn Effect: Does Carbon Fixing Offer a New Escape from the Bogey of Compound Interest?', *Forestry Chronicle*, pp. 572-577

Quirk, Peter J. *et al* (1987), *Floating Exchange Rates in Developing Countries: Experience with Auction and Interbank Markets*, Occasional Paper no. 53, IMF, Washington, DC.

Rahman, A. (1986), *Peasants and Classes: a study in differentiation in Bangladesh*, London, Zed Press.

Ravindranath, N.H. and Somashekar, B.S. (1994), 'Potential and Economics of Forestry Options for Carbon Sequestration in India', *Biomass and Bioenergy*, vol. 8, no. 5, pp. 323-336.

Reddy, C.R. (1985), 'Rural Labour Market in Varhad : A Case Study of Agricultural Labourers in Rain-Fed Agriculture in India', Working Paper, no. WEP 10-6/WP75, International Labour Office, Geneva.

Reddy, S.R.C. (1998), *User Group Benefit Appropriation in the Global Commons: An Economic Analysis of Tropical Forest Management under Uncertainty with a Case Study of India*, PhD thesis, University of Wales, Bangor (UK).

Reddy, S.R.C. and Chakravarty, S.P. (1999), 'Forest Dependence and Income Distribution in a Subsistence Economy: Evidence from India', World Development, vol. 27, no. 7, pp. 1141-1149.

Rogaly, B. (1996), 'Agricultural Growth and the Structure of 'Casual' Labour-Hiring in Rural West Bengal', Journal of Peasant Studies, vol. 23, no. 4, pp. 141-65.

Rogaly, B. (1997), 'Dangerous Liaisons? Seasonal Labour Migration and Agrarian Change in West Bengal' in Rogaly, B., Harriss-White, B. and Bose, S. (ed.) Sonar Bangla? Agricultural Growth and Agrarian Change in West Bengal and Bangladesh (forthcoming).

Rondinelli, D.A (1995), 'Privatisation and economic transformation: The management challenge', in Prokopenko, J. (ed.), Management for Privatisation, International labour office, Geneva.

Rothbarth, E. (1940), 'The Measurement of Changes in Real Income under Conditions of Rationing', Review of Economic Studies, vol. 8, pp. 100-107.

Roy, R. (1996), 'State Failure in India: Political-Fiscal Implications of the Black Economy', IDS Bulletin, vol. 27, no. 2, pp. 22-30.

Sandler, Todd (1993), 'A Tropical Deforestation: Markets and Market Failures', Land Economics, vol. 69, No. 3, August, pp. 225-233.

Sanker, T.L., Mishra R.K. and Mohammed, L.S. (1994), 'Divestments in public enterprises: The Indian Experience', International Journal of Public Sector Management, vol. 7, no 2, pp. 69-88.

Sarayadar, Edward (1983), 'Bargaining Power, Dissimulation and the Coase Theorem', Journal of Institutional and Theoretical Economics, vol. 139, pp. 599-611.

Schmidt, P. and Strauss, R. P. (1975), 'The Prediction of Occupation Using Multiple Logit Models', International Economic Review, p. 471-86.

Scott, C.D. and Litchfield, J. A. (1994), 'Inequality, Mobility and the Determinants of Income Among the Rural Poor in Chile, 1968-86', Discussion Paper no. 53, Development Economics Research Programme, STICERD, London School of Economics.

Sedjo R.A. and Solomon A.M. (1989), 'Climate and Forest', pp. 105-120 in Rosenberg, N.J., Easterling, W.E., Crosson, P.R. and Darmstadter, J. (eds), Greenhouse Warming: Abatement and Adaptation, RFF Proceedings, Washington, D. C.: Resources for the Future.

Sen, Amartya (1975), Employment, Technology and Development, Clarendon Press, Oxford.

Sen, Amartya and Sunil Sengupta (1983), 'Malnutrition of Rural Children and the Sex Bias', Economic and Political Weekly, 19 (Annual Number).

Sengupta, Sunil and Gazdar, H. (1997), 'Agrarian Politics and Rural Development in West Bengal', in Dreze and Sen (eds), *Indian Development: Selected Regional Perspectives*, Oxford University Press, Oxford and New Delhi.

Shanin, T. (1972), *The Awkward Class*, Penguin.

Sheik, A. Munir (1976), 'Black Market for Foreign Exchange, Capital Flows and Smuggling', *Journal of Development Economics*, vol. 3, p. 9-26.

Storm, S. (1997), 'Domestic Constraints on Export-Led Growth: A Case Study of India', *Journal of Development Economics*, vol. 52, no. 1, pp. 82-119.

Thakur, R. (1996), 'India and the United States', *Asian Survey*, vol. 36, no. 6, pp. 574-591.

Tobin, J. and Houthakker, H.S. (1950), 'The Effects of Rationing on Demand Elasticities', *Review of Economic Studies*, vol. 18, p. 140-153.

Tol, R.S.J. (1995), 'The Damage Costs of Climate Change: Towards More Comprehensive Calculations', *Environmental and Resource Economics*, vol. 5, pp. 353-374.

United Nations (1973, 1985, 1992) *International Commodity Trade Statistics*, U.N., New York.

Vaidyanathan, A. (1989), 'Macro and Micro Approaches to Studying Rural Economic Change: Some Pointers from Indian Experience', in Bardhan, P. (ed), *Conversations between Economists and Anthropologists: Methodological Issues in Measuring Economic Change in Rural India*, Oxford University Press, Delhi.

Van Schendel, W. (1981), *Peasant Mobility: The odds of life in rural Bangladesh*, Assen: van Gorcum.

Vickers, J. and Yarrow, G. (1988), *Privatisation: An Economic Analysis*, Cambridge, MA: MIT Press.

Walker, R. (1995), 'The dynamics of poverty and social exclusion', in G. Room (ed), *Beyond the Threshold: the Measurement and Analysis of Social Exclusion*, The Policy Press, WIDER 1989, Bristol.

Walker, T.S. and Ryan, J.G. (1990), *Village and Household Economies in India's Semi-arid Tropics*, John Hopkins University Press, Baltimore and London.

World Bank (1992), 'Issues for Infrastructure Management in the 1990s', *World Bank Discussion papers*, 171.

World Bank (1992), 'Strategy for Forest Sector Development in Asia, World Bank Technical Paper 182, Asia Technical Department Series', World Bank, Washington, D. C.

World Bank (1993), 'Telecommunications - World Bank Experience and Strategy', *World Bank Discussion Papers*, 192.

World Bank (1994), *Trends in Developing Countries*, Washington, DC.

World Bank (1994a), *World Development Report 1994*, Washington, DC: World Bank.

World Bank (1994b), 'Telecommunications Sector Reform in Asia - Towards a New Pragmatism', *World Bank Discussion papers*, 232.

Xu, D. (1994), 'The Potential for Reducing Atmospheric Carbon by Large Scale Afforestation in China and Related Cost/Benefit Analysis', *Biomass and Bioenergy*, vol. 8, no. 5, pp. 337-344.

Yampoin, R. and Kerr, W.A. (1996), *Suppressing the New Pirates: Protection of Intellectual Property Rights in Asia - A Challenge for the World Trade Organization*, EPRI Report, no. 96-01, Excellence in the Pacific Research Institute, University of Lethbridge, Lethbridge, Canada.

Yeung, M., Kerr, W.A. and Perdikis, N. (1997), *Like Ships Passing in the Night: Relations Between ASEAN and the European Union*, EPRI Report no. 97-02, Excellence in the Pacific Research Institute, University of Lethbridge, Lethbridge, Canada.

Index

For Product Safety Concerns and Information please contact our EU
representative GPSR@taylorandfrancis.com Taylor & Francis Verlag GmbH,
Kaufingerstraße 24, 80331 München, Germany

Printed and bound by CPI Group (UK) Ltd, Croydon, CR0 4YY
01/05/2025
01858342-0006